NEGATIVE
SPACE™

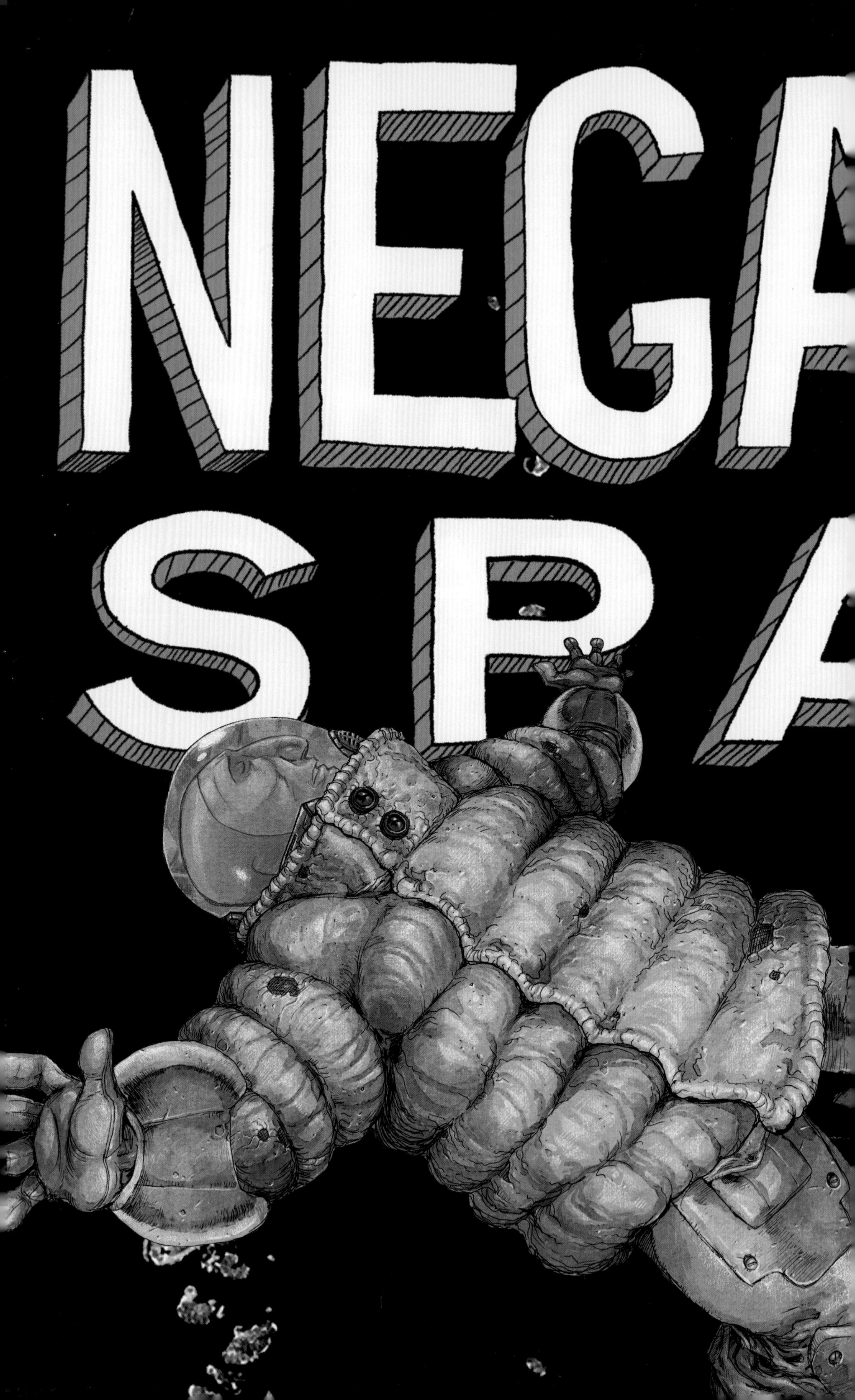
NEGA
SPA

ATIVE
ACE ™

Script by
RYAN K LINDSAY

Art by
OWEN GIENI

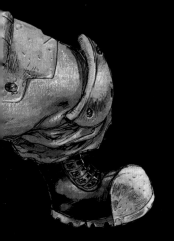

Letters by **Ryan Ferrier**

Cover art and chapter breaks by
Owen Gieni

DARK HORSE BOOKS

President & Publisher, Mike Richardson · Editor, Daniel Chabon · Assistant Editors, Ian Tucker & Cardner Clark · Designer, Justin Couch · Digital Art Technician, Christina McKenzie

First edition: July 2016
ISBN 978-1-61655-886-4

10 9 8 7 6 5 4 3 2 1

Published by Dark Horse Books, a division of Dark Horse Comics, Inc. 10956 SE Main Street, Milwaukie, OR 97222

This volume collects issues #1–#4 of the Dark Horse Comics series *Negative Space*.

Library of Congress Cataloging-in-Publication Data

Names: Lindsay, Ryan K., author. | Gieni, Owen, illustrator. | Ferrier, Ryan, illustrator.
Title: Negative space / script by Ryan K Lindsay ; art by Owen Gieni ; letters by Ryan Ferrier ; cover art and chapter breaks by Owen Gieni.
Description: First edition. | Milwaukie, OR : Dark Horse Books, 2016. | "A suicidal writer uncovers a conspiracy dedicated to creating and mining the worst lows of human desperation. He partners with a cult intent on exposing the corporation that has been selling human sadness to ancient underwater creatures, and goes on a suicide mission to stop it"--Provided by publisher.
Identifiers: LCCN 2015034573 | ISBN 9781616558864 (paperback)
Subjects: LCSH: Graphic novels. | Comic books, strips, etc. | BISAC: COMICS & GRAPHIC NOVELS / Horror.
Classification: LCC PN6727.L536 N44 2016 | DDC 741.5/973--dc23
LC record available at http://lccn.loc.gov/2015034573

To find a comics shop in your area, call the Comic Shop Locator Service toll-free at 1-888-266-4226.
International Licensing: (503) 905-2377

DarkHorse.com

1
DEPRESSION AGENCY
2
THE
DEPRESSION AGENCY
3
THE
AGENCY
4
THE DEPRESSION AGENCY
1

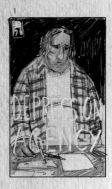

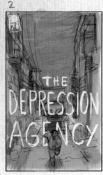

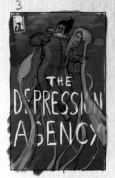

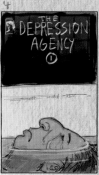

INTRODUCTION

by Christopher Sebela

I drove out to my favorite bridge the other night to kill myself.

The St. Johns Bridge is clear on the other side of Portland from me, but it's a marvel of design, a beautiful thing even to someone who doesn't fawn over architecture. In my head, I thought, "Gee, I've never seen it at night, though," as I got in my car and pointed myself toward it at 9:30. Heavy rain was coming down, and I was at the tail end of what had proven to be a relentlessly bad day coming at the end of some relentlessly bad weeks. Sometimes that's all it takes: a quirk of circumstance and timing, and here come those old bastards in my head, the patron saints of self-oblivion who, it turns out, never move out, only burrow deeper out of sight.

After a long drive to the bridge, I cruised slowly across it (*just to see, just to see*, I told myself), then turned around and crossed it again, finally completing one last circuit, to make absolutely sure. It was quiet, foggy, not heavily trafficked out here where everyone seems to be in bed by 10:01 p.m. Nothing in the world was stopping me from pulling over, throwing my door open, and going for a running leap off the railing. A few seconds of regret and then nothing at all.

Spoiler: I didn't this time. I had excuses. Reasons why not. I had guests coming in from out of town. I had deadlines. It was Christmas soon. I needed more time. But I figure it's always good to do your homework for that moment when a single excuse for why not no longer comes to mind. Sometimes it's a story you tell yourself to feel better when everything else is flaming garbage as far as you can see.

Maybe this is why I like *Negative Space* as much as I do. Because it takes these queasy, quiet urges and strips them of their nebulousness, giving them motives, appetites, names, and faces. Dressing up the deep, dark holes of human emotion in a bureaucratic structure, all wrapped in the gallows-est humor possible. Ryan Lindsay ably expands what might be a depressing one-liner into an epic that slyly moves from dramatic character study to fantastical sci-fi horror story and back again.

There's a hopeful recognition in Guy. He's clearly driven to the end of his rope by forces beyond his control—huge multinationals that get rich on the backs of human misery, driven on by the idea of a world-saving mission against eldritch monsters who know a bargain when they see one. But it's not his fault. The world and all the beauty in it can turn on a dime and become bloody and sad because someone pushes a button. All of it is achingly given life by Owen Gieni, who can note each little crack of a smile or crushing misery on a human face as easily as he can pose the jaunty tentacles of a monster hiding in a puffy coat or cover a page in psychedelic emotional-turmoil waves.

Negative Space paints the world around us, the world beneath that world we never see, and the world inside us that others rarely do. We're each of us Guy, on the verge of departing; Woody, the earnest struggler; Rick, the bastard efficiency; Briggs, the quiet opportunist. The universe is full of love and full of horrors, and the only choice we really have is to fight back against it or give in to it, even when the signs overhead are burned out and we don't know which is the right choice anymore.

Sometimes that choice is a bridge. Most times, if you're lucky, it's just a story you can see yourself in even as it swallows you up. *Negative Space* is one of those stories. Hide your car keys; make yourself comfortable. The world, all your hard decisions, and every black hole in it will still be here when you're done.

Christopher Sebela
Portland, OR
December 30, 2015

STRANGER

KINDRED
SOLDIER

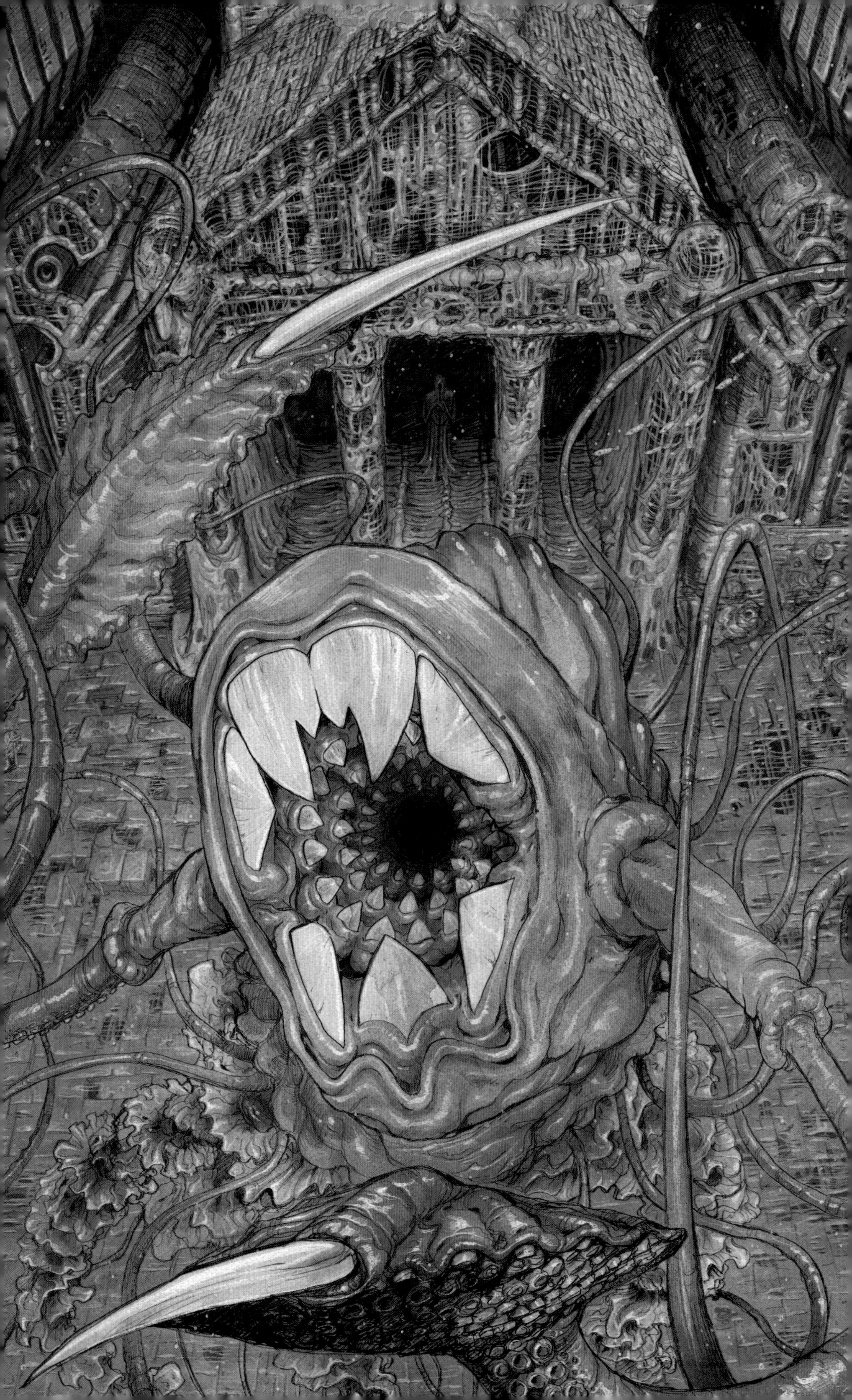

Exhibit 015
Helen Rigby's Diary

Helen Rigby wrote a poem a day for her entire adult life. Most of these sonnets were directed at a married man whom she loved secretly. He was the town undertaker, and as she took her own life, she held the book, knowing he'd finally read it after taking it from her cold hands. His wife found it first, read it, laughed, and gave it to the Evorah monsters.

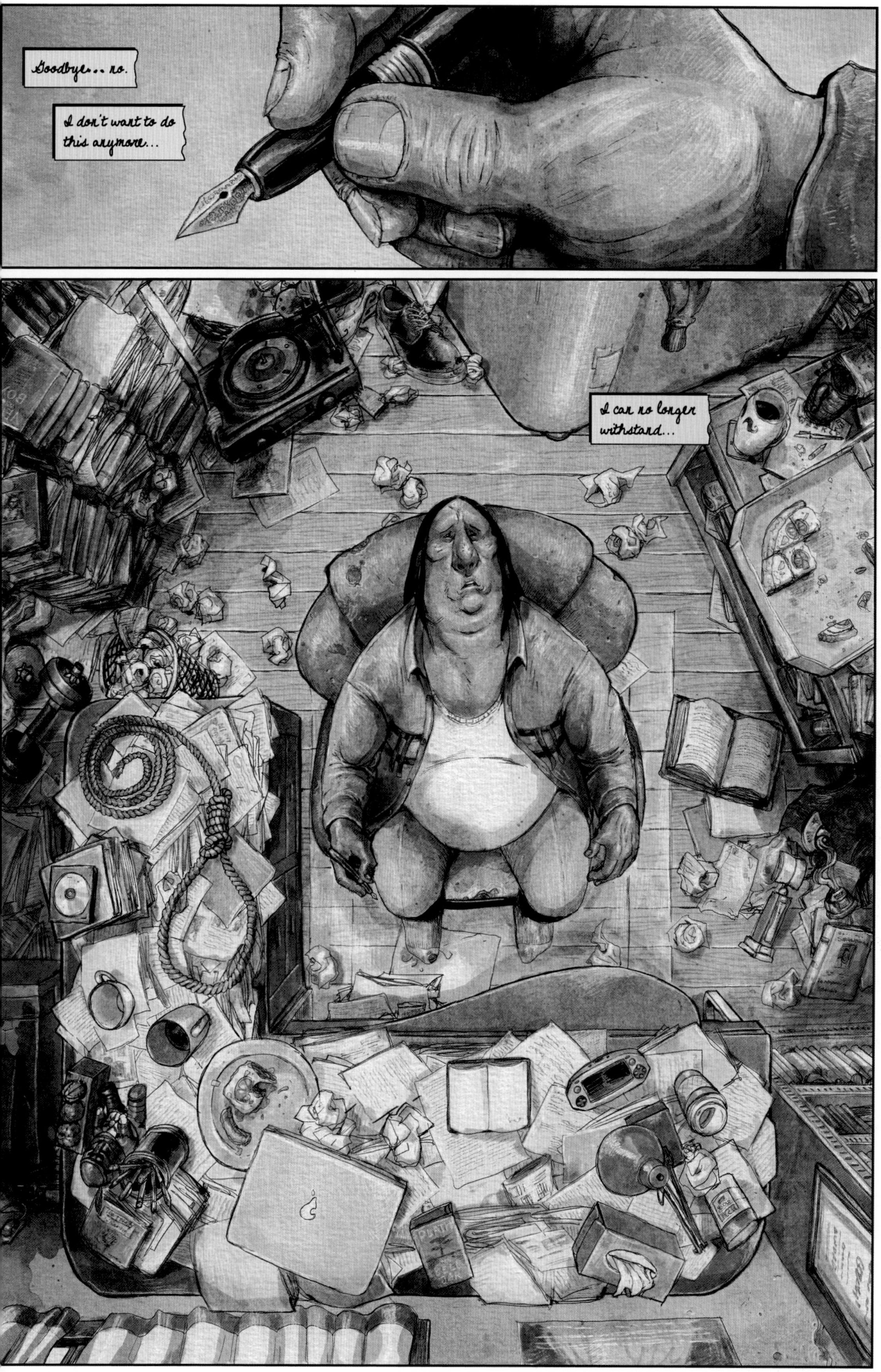
Goodbye... no.
I don't want to do this anymore...
I can no longer withstand...

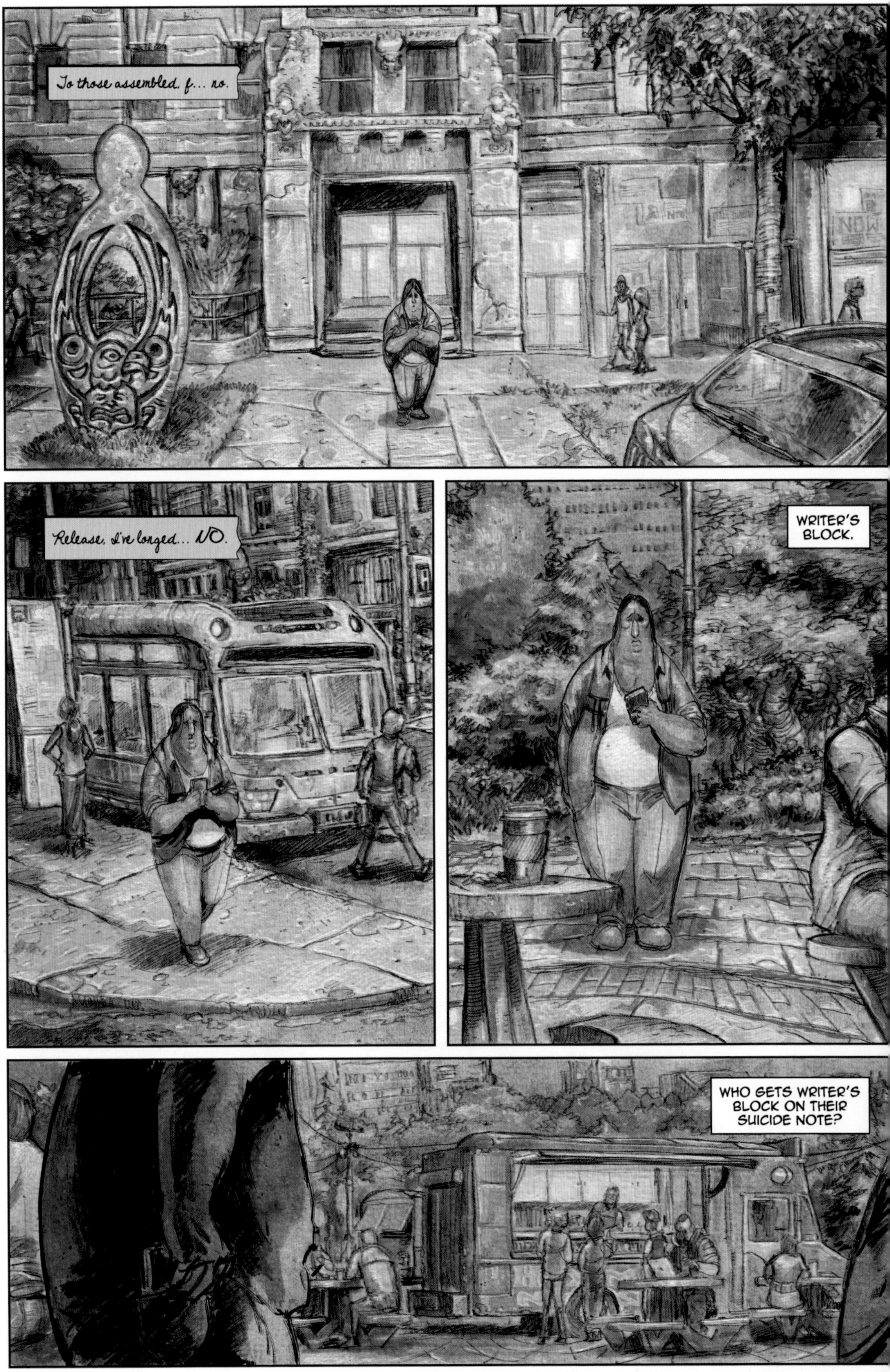
To those assembled, f... no.
Release, I've longed... NO.
WRITER'S BLOCK.
WHO GETS WRITER'S BLOCK ON THEIR SUICIDE NOTE?

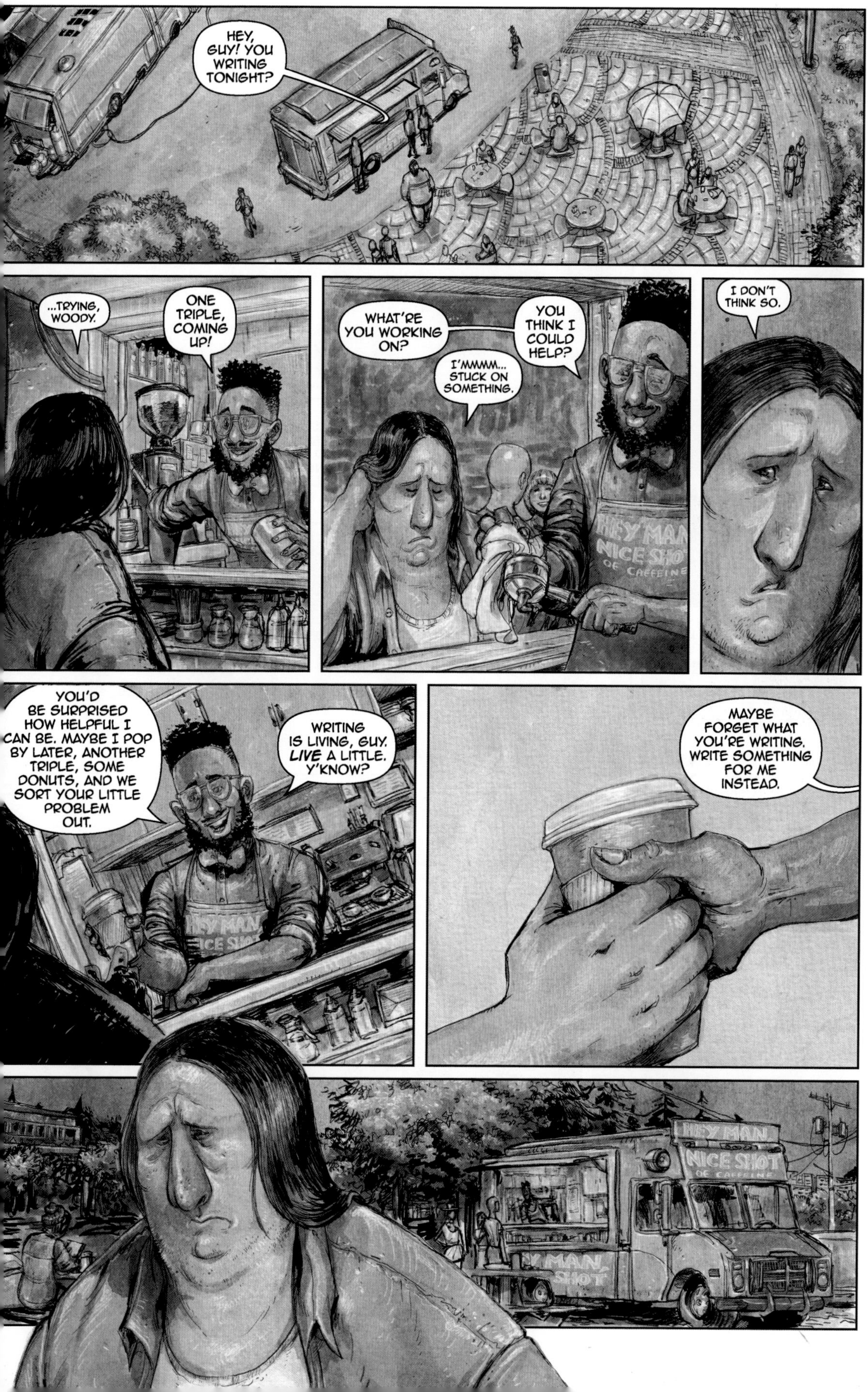
HEY, GUY! YOU WRITING TONIGHT?
...TRYING, WOODY.
ONE TRIPLE, COMING UP!
WHAT'RE YOU WORKING ON?
YOU THINK I COULD HELP?
I'MMMM... STUCK ON SOMETHING.
I DON'T THINK SO.
YOU'D BE SURPRISED HOW HELPFUL I CAN BE. MAYBE I POP BY LATER, ANOTHER TRIPLE, SOME DONUTS, AND WE SORT YOUR LITTLE PROBLEM OUT.
WRITING IS LIVING, GUY. LIVE A LITTLE. Y'KNOW?
MAYBE FORGET WHAT YOU'RE WRITING. WRITE SOMETHING FOR ME INSTEAD.
HEY MAN, NICE SHOT OF CAFFEINE

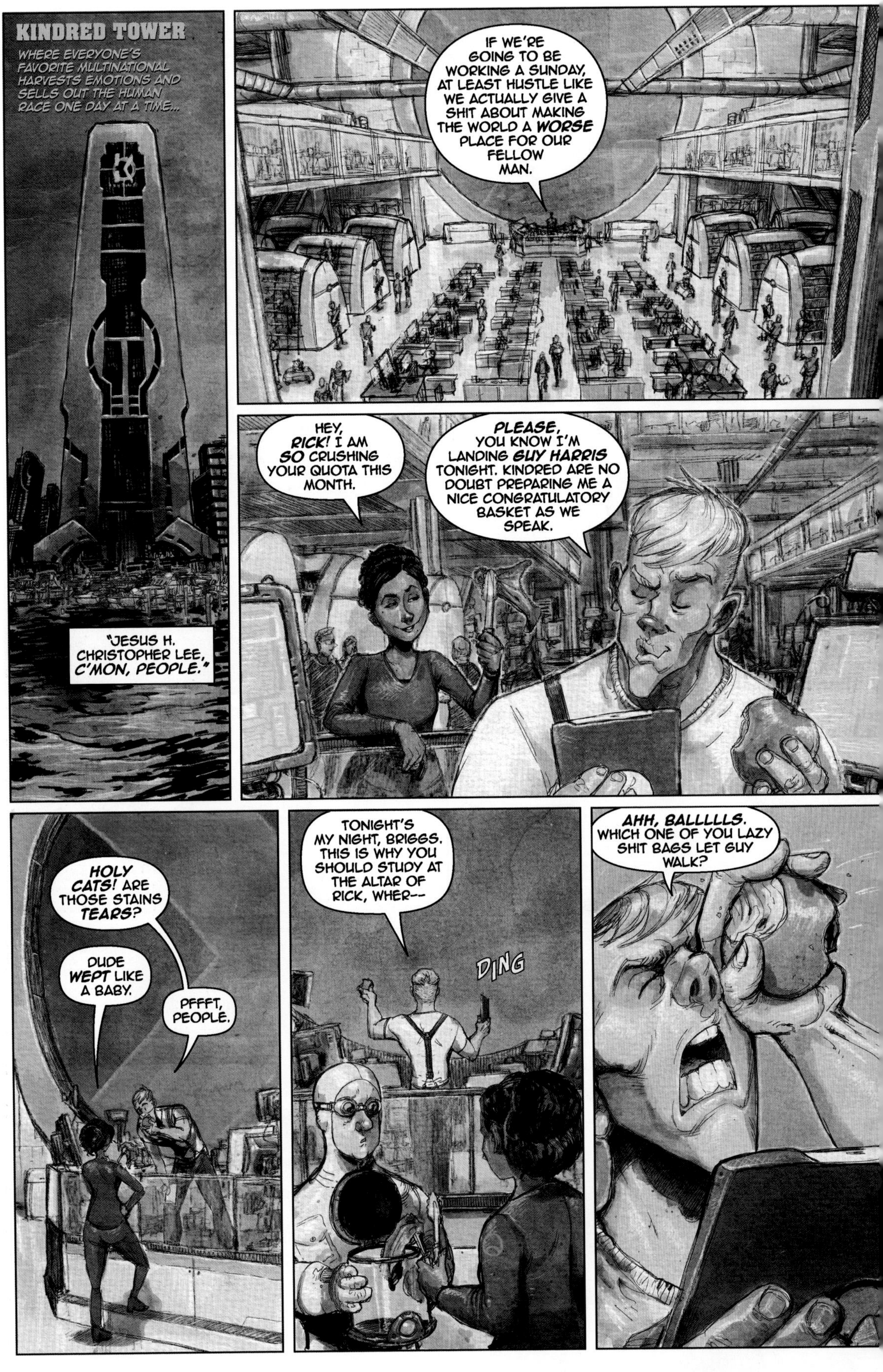
KINDRED TOWER
WHERE EVERYONE'S FAVORITE MULTINATIONAL HARVESTS EMOTIONS AND SELLS OUT THE HUMAN RACE ONE DAY AT A TIME...
"JESUS H. CHRISTOPHER LEE, C'MON, PEOPLE."
IF WE'RE GOING TO BE WORKING A SUNDAY, AT LEAST HUSTLE LIKE WE ACTUALLY GIVE A SHIT ABOUT MAKING THE WORLD A WORSE PLACE FOR OUR FELLOW MAN.
HEY, RICK! I AM SO CRUSHING YOUR QUOTA THIS MONTH.
PLEASE, YOU KNOW I'M LANDING GUY HARRIS TONIGHT. KINDRED ARE NO DOUBT PREPARING ME A NICE CONGRATULATORY BASKET AS WE SPEAK.
HOLY CATS! ARE THOSE STAINS TEARS?
DUDE WEPT LIKE A BABY.
PFFFT, PEOPLE.
TONIGHT'S MY NIGHT, BRIGGS. THIS IS WHY YOU SHOULD STUDY AT THE ALTAR OF RICK, WHER--
DING
AHH, BALLLLLS. WHICH ONE OF YOU LAZY SHIT BAGS LET GUY WALK?

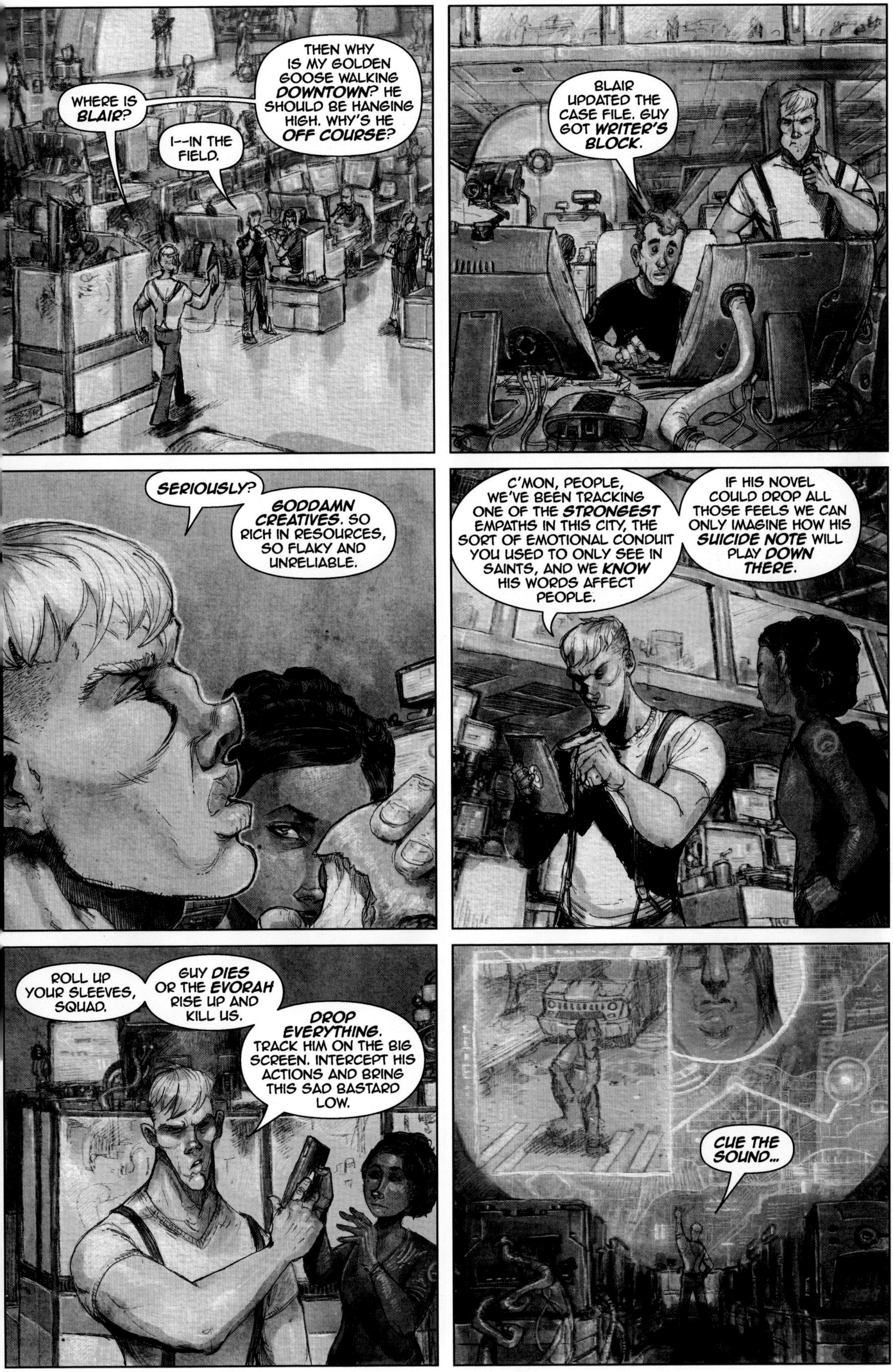
WHERE IS BLAIR?
THEN WHY IS MY GOLDEN GOOSE WALKING DOWNTOWN? HE SHOULD BE HANGING HIGH. WHY'S HE OFF COURSE?
I--IN THE FIELD.
BLAIR UPDATED THE CASE FILE. GUY GOT WRITER'S BLOCK.
SERIOUSLY?
GODDAMN CREATIVES. SO RICH IN RESOURCES, SO FLAKY AND UNRELIABLE.
C'MON, PEOPLE, WE'VE BEEN TRACKING ONE OF THE STRONGEST EMPATHS IN THIS CITY, THE SORT OF EMOTIONAL CONDUIT YOU USED TO ONLY SEE IN SAINTS, AND WE KNOW HIS WORDS AFFECT PEOPLE.
IF HIS NOVEL COULD DROP ALL THOSE FEELS WE CAN ONLY IMAGINE HOW HIS SUICIDE NOTE WILL PLAY DOWN THERE.
ROLL UP YOUR SLEEVES, SQUAD.
GUY DIES OR THE EVORAH RISE UP AND KILL US.
DROP EVERYTHING. TRACK HIM ON THE BIG SCREEN. INTERCEPT HIS ACTIONS AND BRING THIS SAD BASTARD LOW.
CUE THE SOUND...

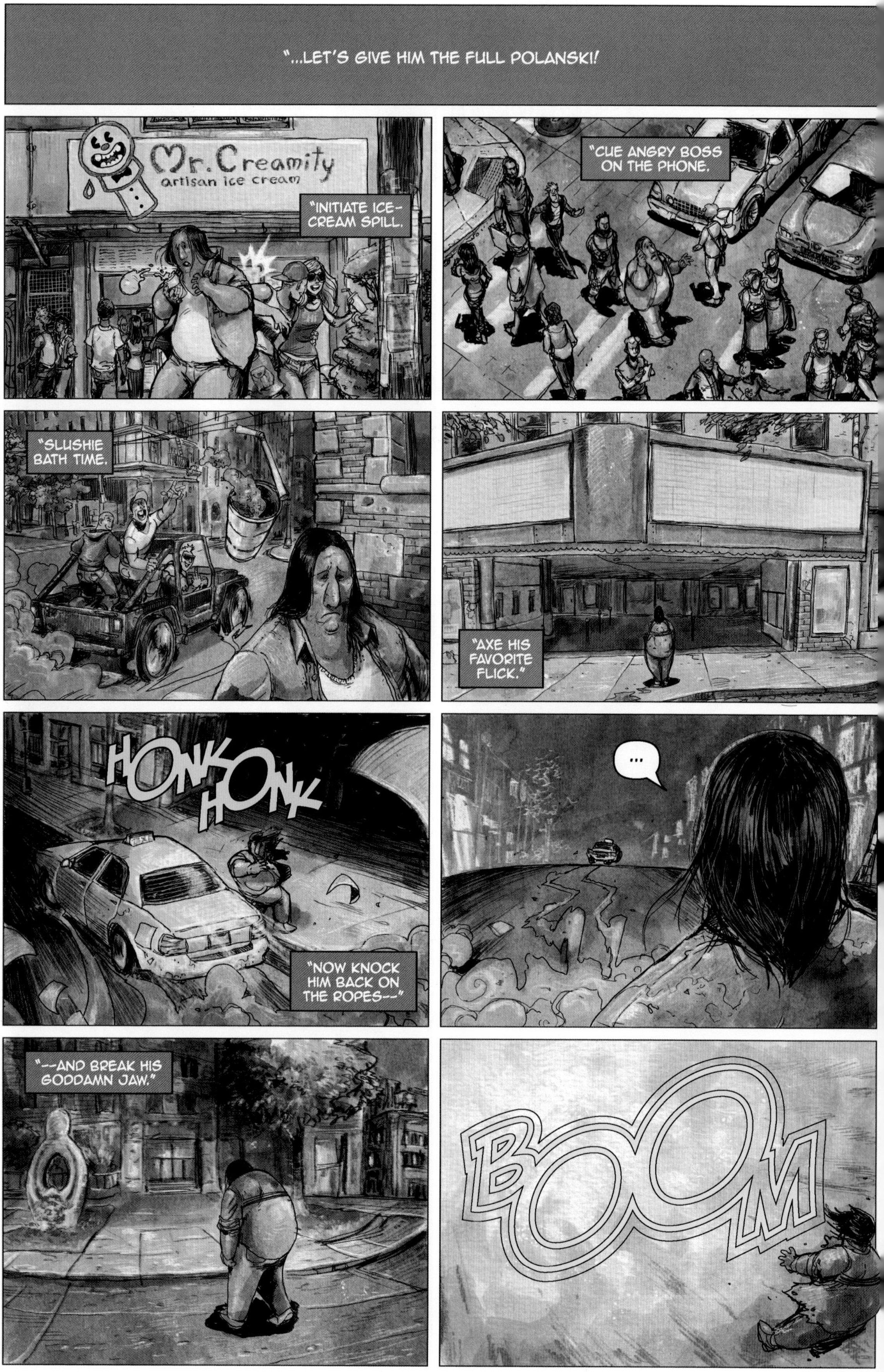
"...LET'S GIVE HIM THE FULL POLANSKI!
Mr. Creamity
artisan ice cream
"INITIATE ICE-CREAM SPILL.
"CUE ANGRY BOSS ON THE PHONE.
"SLUSHIE BATH TIME.
"AXE HIS FAVORITE FLICK."
HONK HONK
"NOW KNOCK HIM BACK ON THE ROPES--"
...
"--AND BREAK HIS GODDAMN JAW."
BOOM

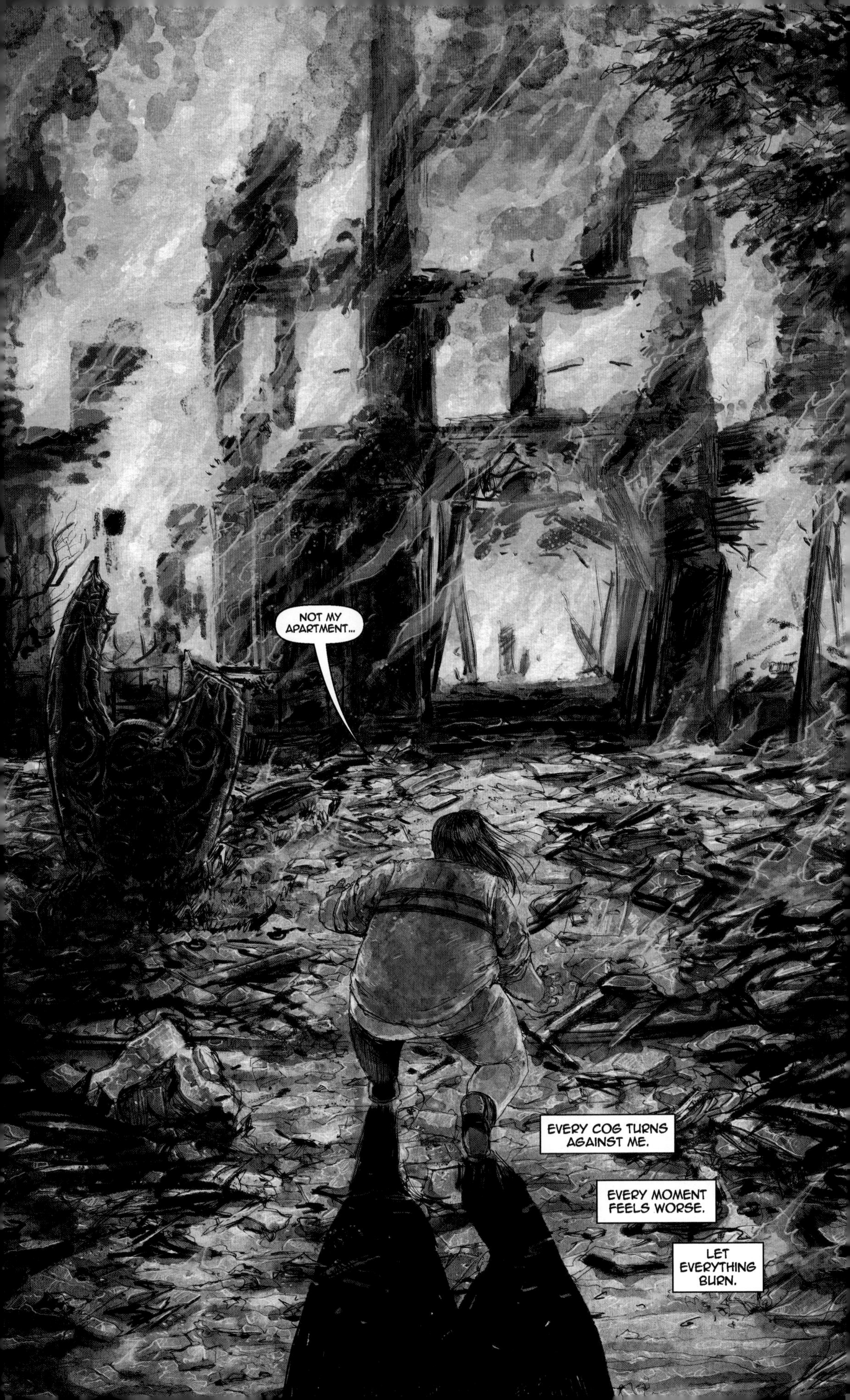
NOT MY APARTMENT...
EVERY COG TURNS AGAINST ME.
EVERY MOMENT FEELS WORSE.
LET EVERYTHING BURN.

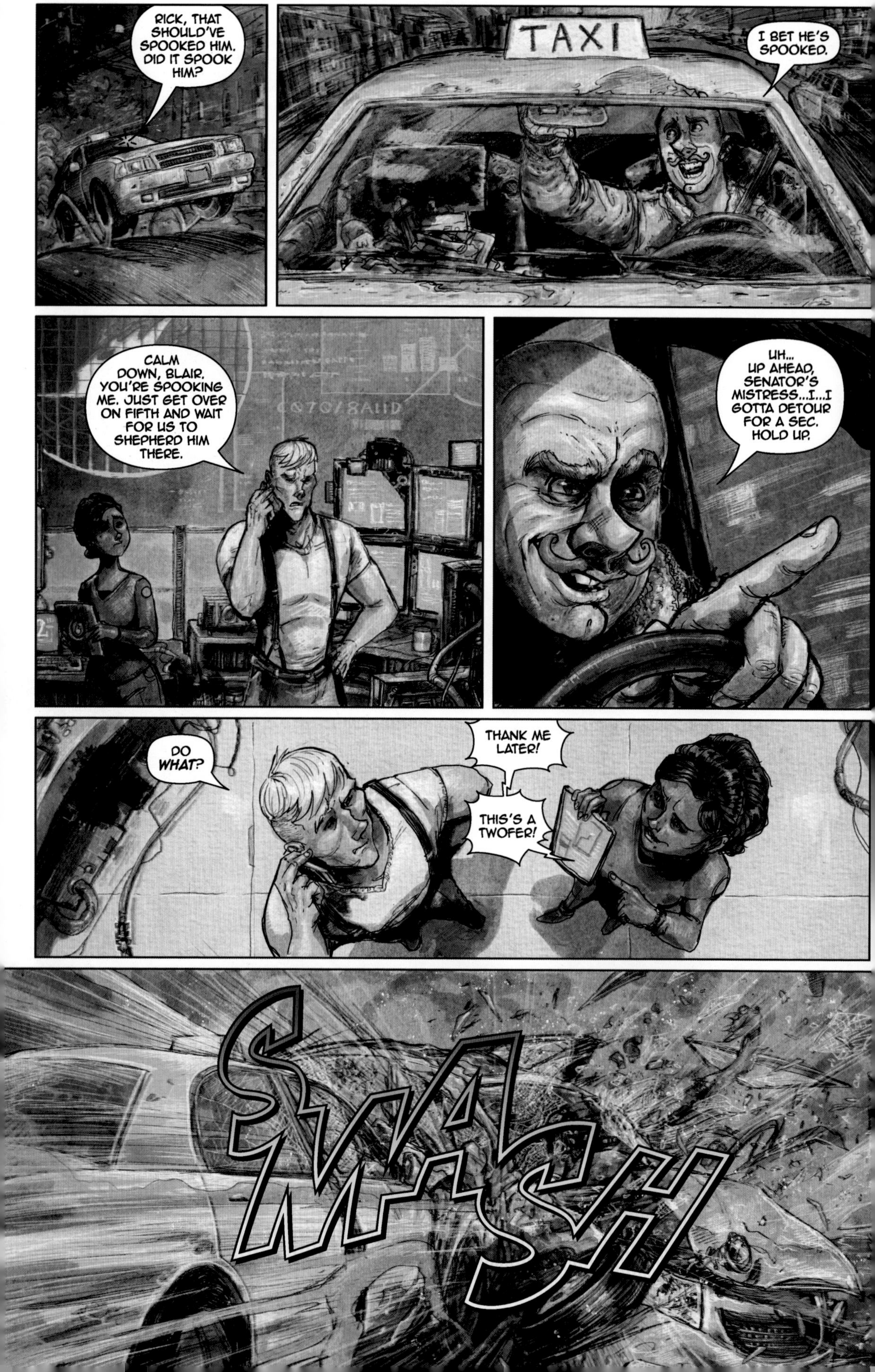
RICK, THAT SHOULD'VE SPOOKED HIM. DID IT SPOOK HIM?
TAXI
I BET HE'S SPOOKED.
CALM DOWN, BLAIR. YOU'RE SPOOKING ME. JUST GET OVER ON FIFTH AND WAIT FOR US TO SHEPHERD HIM THERE.
UH... UP AHEAD, SENATOR'S MISTRESS...I...I GOTTA DETOUR FOR A SEC. HOLD UP.
DO *WHAT?*
THANK ME LATER!
THIS'S A TWOFER!
SMASH

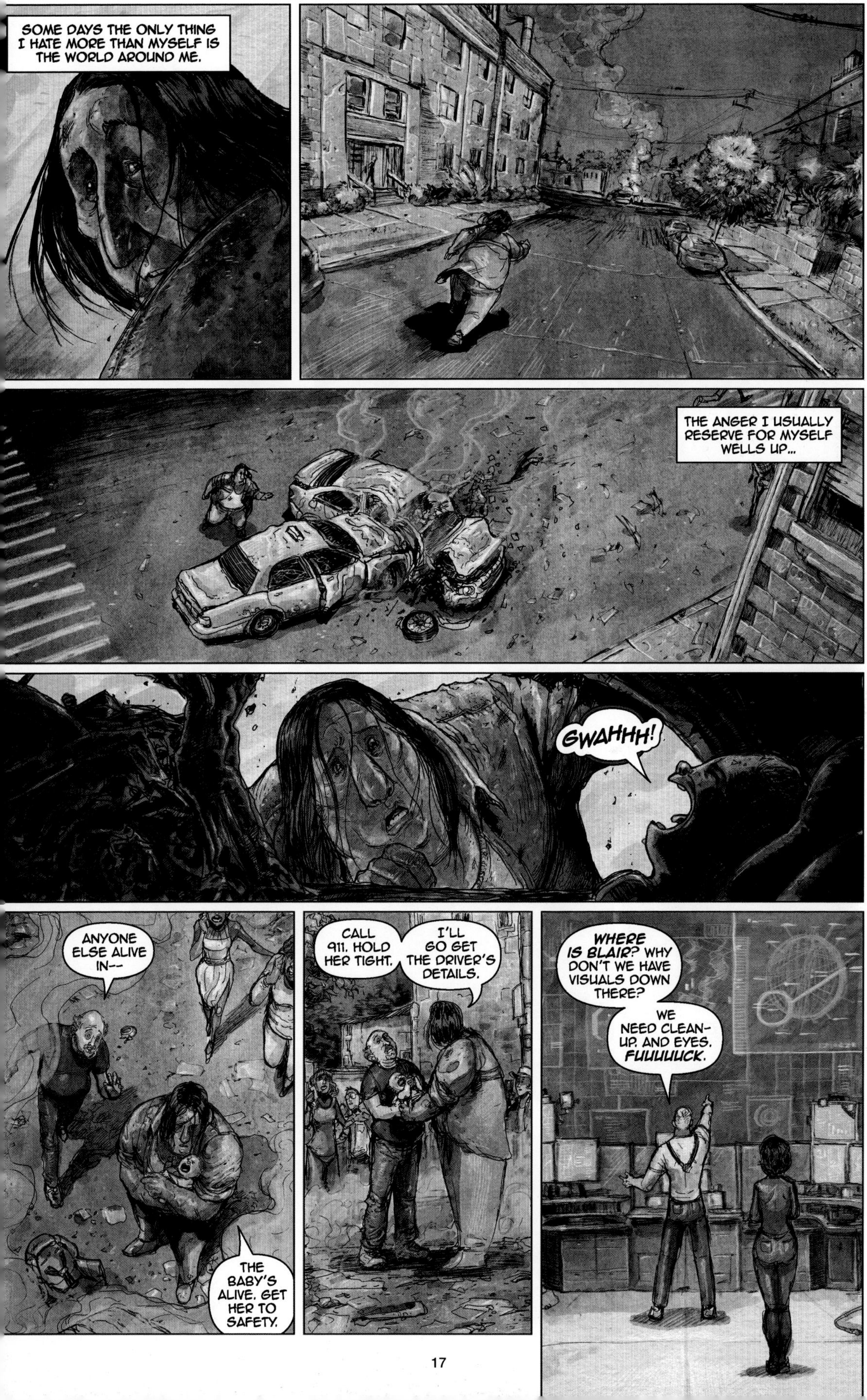
SOME DAYS THE ONLY THING I HATE MORE THAN MYSELF IS THE WORLD AROUND ME.
THE ANGER I USUALLY RESERVE FOR MYSELF WELLS UP...
GWAHHH!
ANYONE ELSE ALIVE IN--
THE BABY'S ALIVE. GET HER TO SAFETY.
CALL 911. HOLD HER TIGHT.
I'LL GO GET THE DRIVER'S DETAILS.
WHERE IS BLAIR? WHY DON'T WE HAVE VISUALS DOWN THERE?
WE NEED CLEAN-UP. AND EYES. FUUUUUCK.

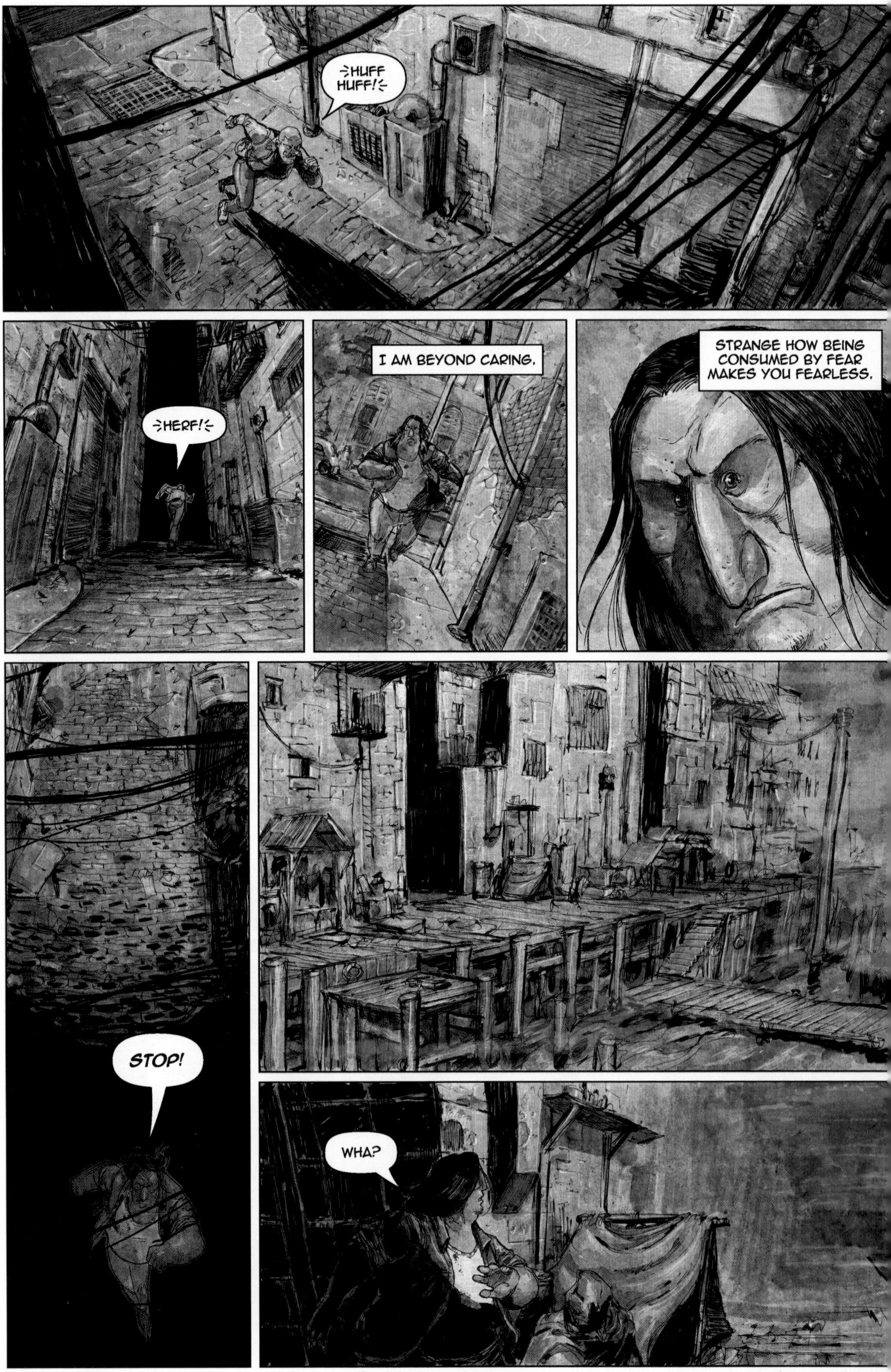
HUFF HUFF!
HERF!
I AM BEYOND CARING.
STRANGE HOW BEING CONSUMED BY FEAR MAKES YOU FEARLESS.
STOP!
WHA?

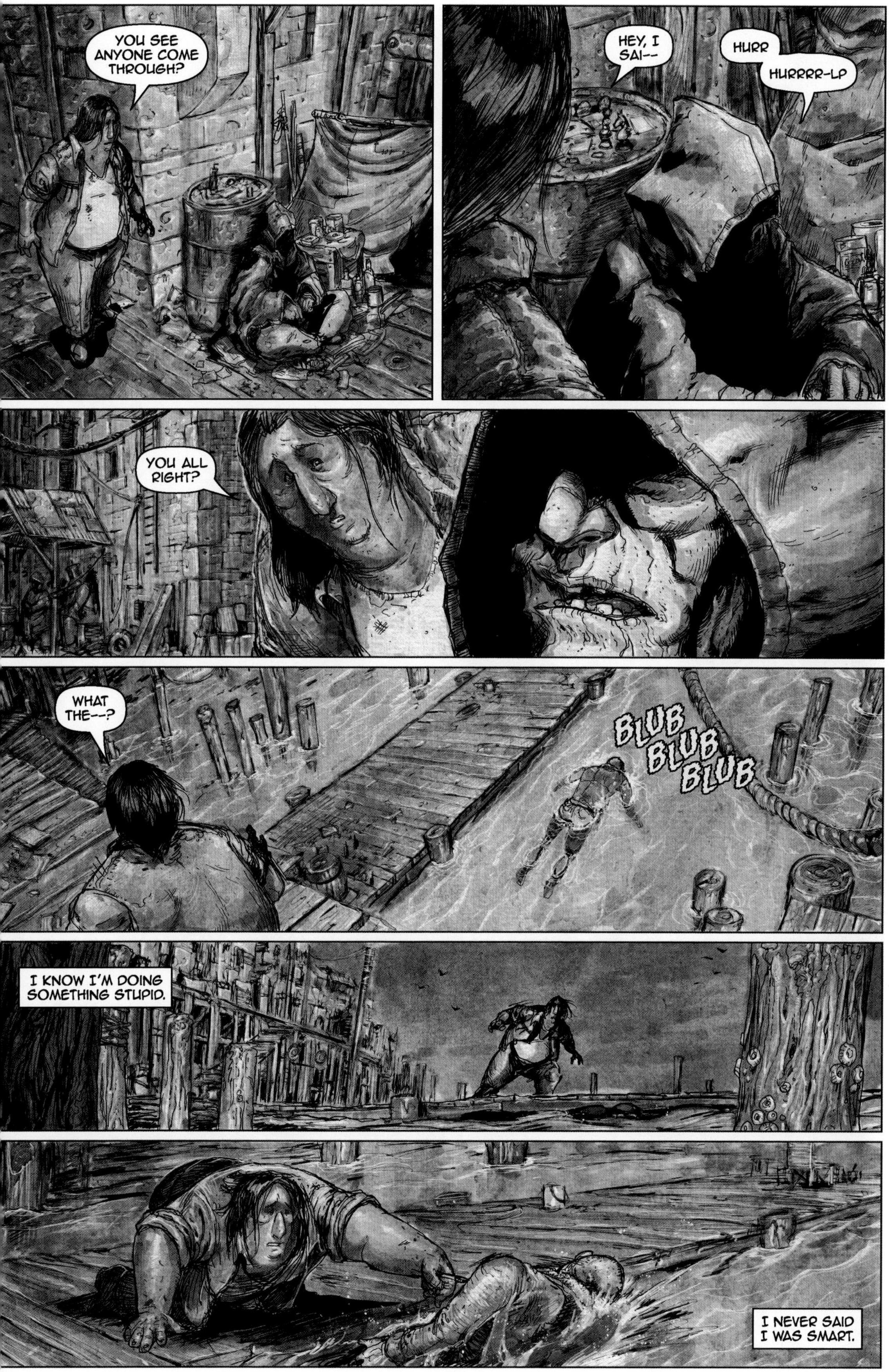
YOU SEE ANYONE COME THROUGH?
HEY, I SAI--
HURR
HURRRR-LP
YOU ALL RIGHT?
WHAT THE--?
BLUB BLUB BLUB
I KNOW I'M DOING SOMETHING STUPID.
I NEVER SAID I WAS SMART.

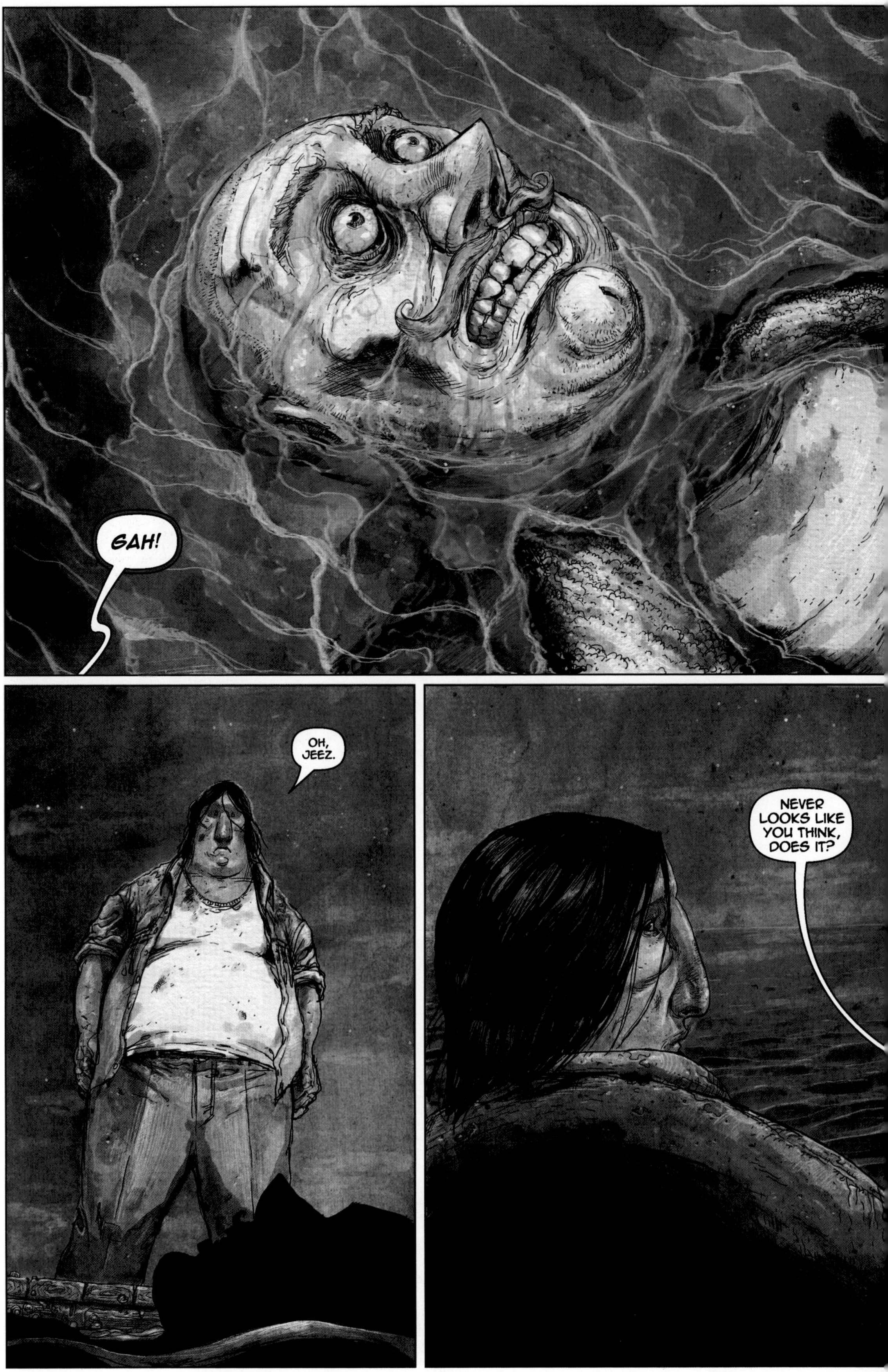
GAH!
OH, JEEZ.
NEVER LOOKS LIKE YOU THINK, DOES IT?

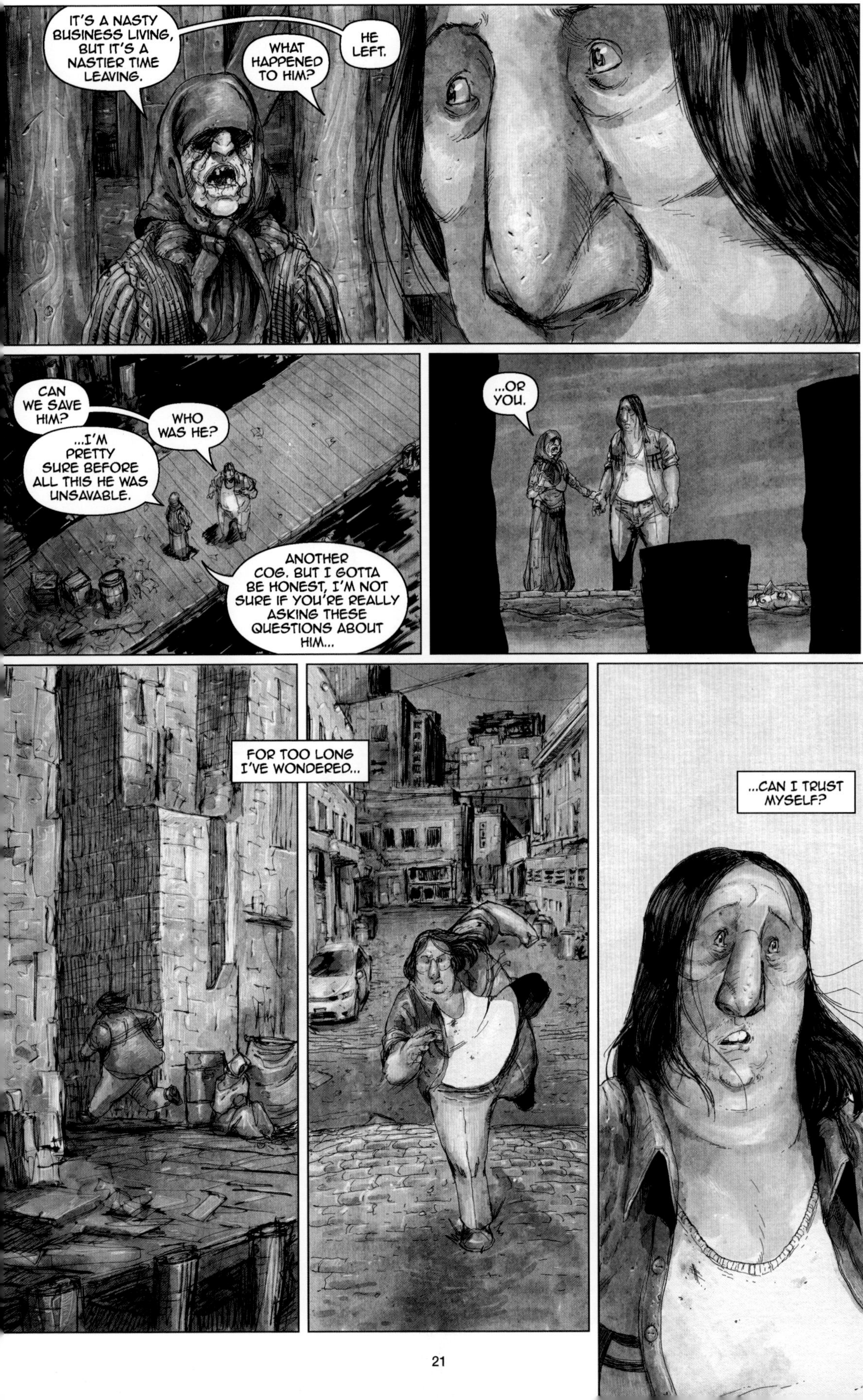
IT'S A NASTY BUSINESS LIVING, BUT IT'S A NASTIER TIME LEAVING.
WHAT HAPPENED TO HIM?
HE LEFT.
CAN WE SAVE HIM?
WHO WAS HE?
...I'M PRETTY SURE BEFORE ALL THIS HE WAS UNSAVABLE.
ANOTHER COG. BUT I GOTTA BE HONEST, I'M NOT SURE IF YOU'RE REALLY ASKING THESE QUESTIONS ABOUT HIM...
...OR YOU.
FOR TOO LONG I'VE WONDERED...
...CAN I TRUST MYSELF?

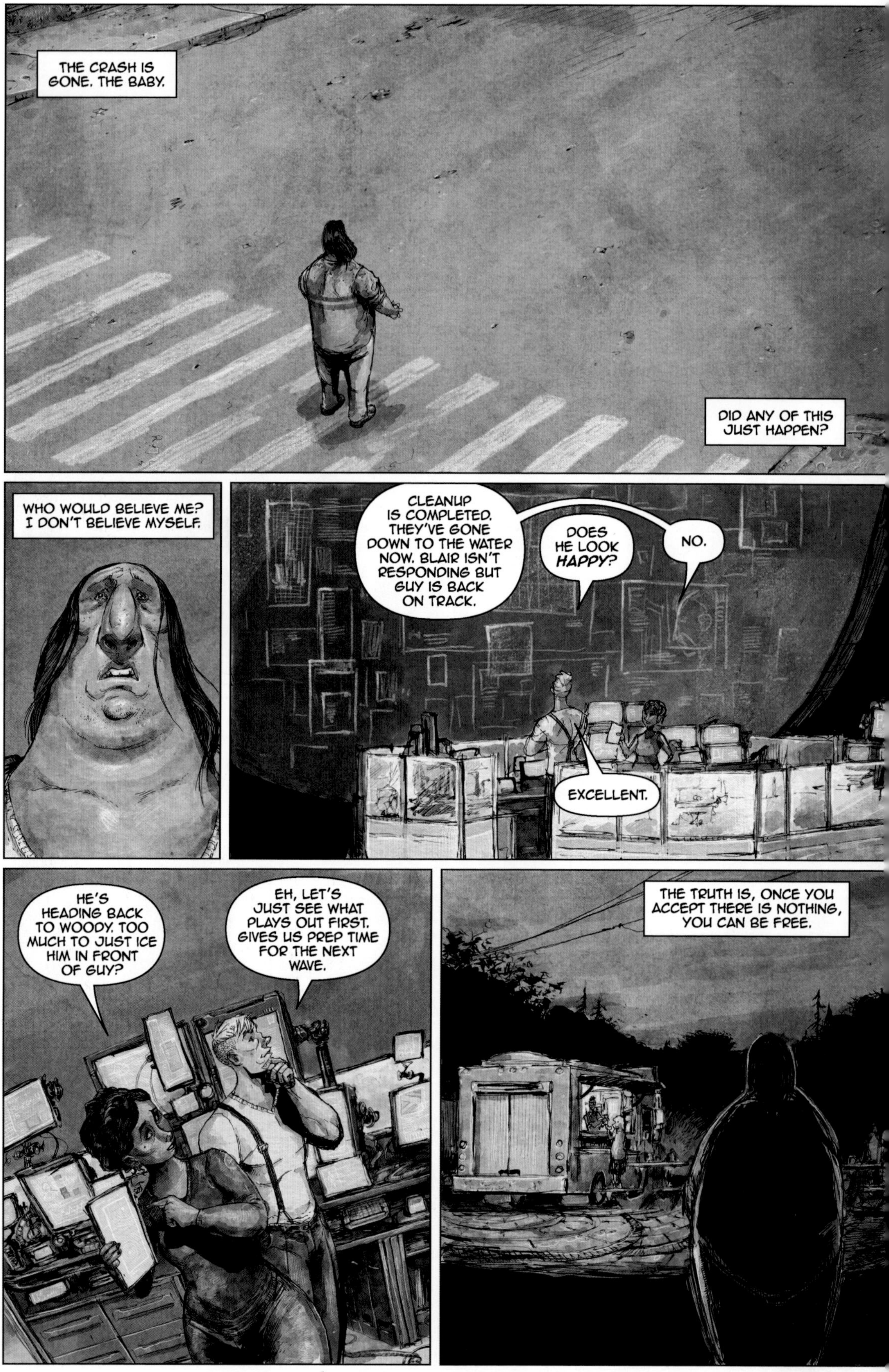
THE CRASH IS GONE. THE BABY.
DID ANY OF THIS JUST HAPPEN?
WHO WOULD BELIEVE ME? I DON'T BELIEVE MYSELF.
CLEANUP IS COMPLETED. THEY'VE GONE DOWN TO THE WATER NOW. BLAIR ISN'T RESPONDING BUT GUY IS BACK ON TRACK.
DOES HE LOOK *HAPPY*?
NO.
EXCELLENT.
HE'S HEADING BACK TO WOODY. TOO MUCH TO JUST ICE HIM IN FRONT OF GUY?
EH, LET'S JUST SEE WHAT PLAYS OUT FIRST. GIVES US PREP TIME FOR THE NEXT WAVE.
THE TRUTH IS, ONCE YOU ACCEPT THERE IS NOTHING, YOU CAN BE FREE.

WOODY, WHAT SCARES YOU?

YOU'RE SCARED OF SPIDERS?

SPIDERS.

AREN'T YOU? ISN'T EVERYBODY?

BIOWARFARE, SIXTEEN-FOOT ANCIENT EGYPTIANS, THE GREATEST EXPANSE OF NOTHING SURROUNDING US FOR LIGHT YEARS, AND THE REST BLASTED BY GAMMA RAYS UNTIL IT'S TOAST.

ALL THAT AND YOU'RE WORRIED ABOUT A SQUASHABLE CREATURE SMALLER THAN YOUR FIST WHOSE SOLE PURPOSE IS TO EAT OTHER, SMALLER BUGS?

LOOK, GUY, YOU ASKED.

TRUE.

YOU KNOW WHAT'S SICK? I GET MOMENTS WHERE I FEEL NO FEAR, IT'S GONE, I'M RELAXED. AND BEING IN THAT STATE SCARES ME THE MOST BECAUSE I'M WORRIED I'VE SWITCHED OFF.

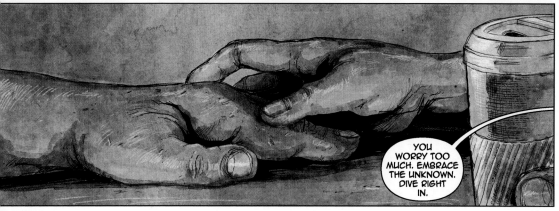

YOU WORRY TOO MUCH. EMBRACE THE UNKNOWN. DIVE RIGHT IN.

I'M GOING TO WRITE SOMETHING FOR YOU. RIGHT NOW.
GREAT!
GREAT!
GUY...UH... ER, I'LL BE RIGHT BACK. RIGHT BACK, OKAY?
HEY MAN NICE SHOT OF CAFFEINE
SURE, NO PROBLEM.

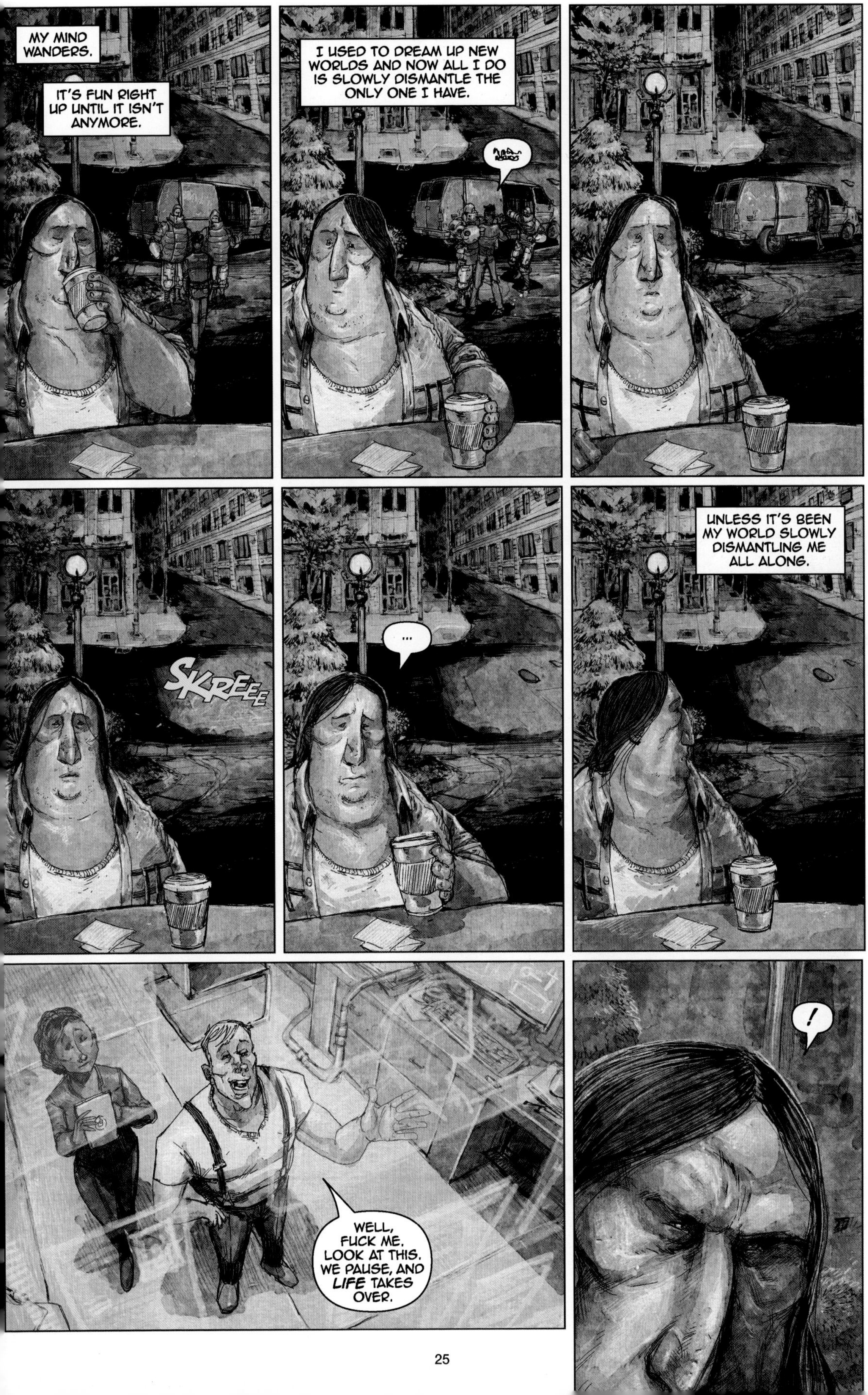
MY MIND WANDERS.
IT'S FUN RIGHT UP UNTIL IT ISN'T ANYMORE.
I USED TO DREAM UP NEW WORLDS AND NOW ALL I DO IS SLOWLY DISMANTLE THE ONLY ONE I HAVE.
SKREEEE
...
UNLESS IT'S BEEN MY WORLD SLOWLY DISMANTLING ME ALL ALONG.
WELL, FUCK ME. LOOK AT THIS. WE PAUSE, AND *LIFE* TAKES OVER.
!

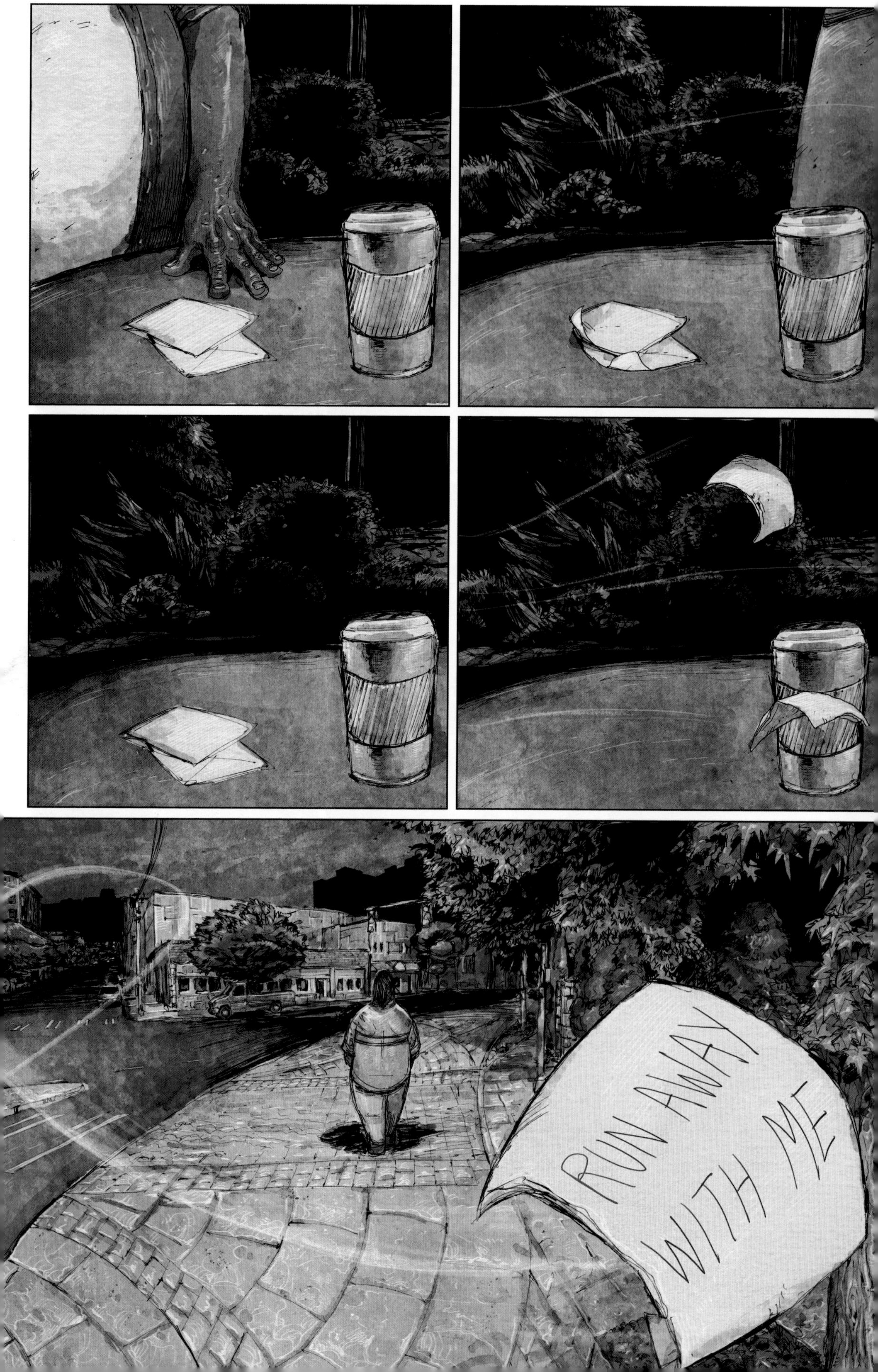
RUN AWAY
WITH ME

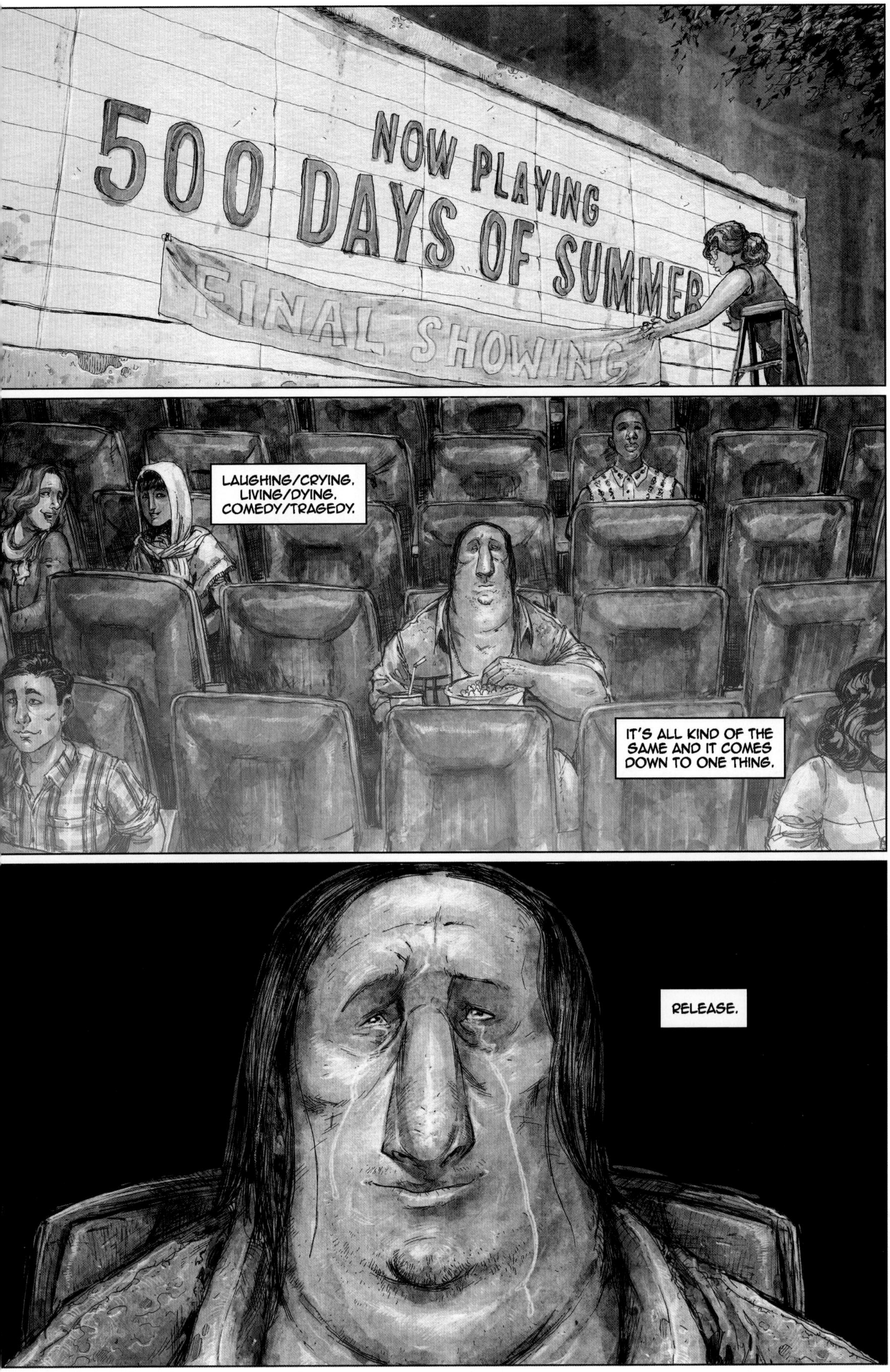
NOW PLAYING
500 DAYS OF SUMMER
FINAL SHOWING
LAUGHING/CRYING.
LIVING/DYING.
COMEDY/TRAGEDY.
IT'S ALL KIND OF THE SAME AND IT COMES DOWN TO ONE THING.
RELEASE.

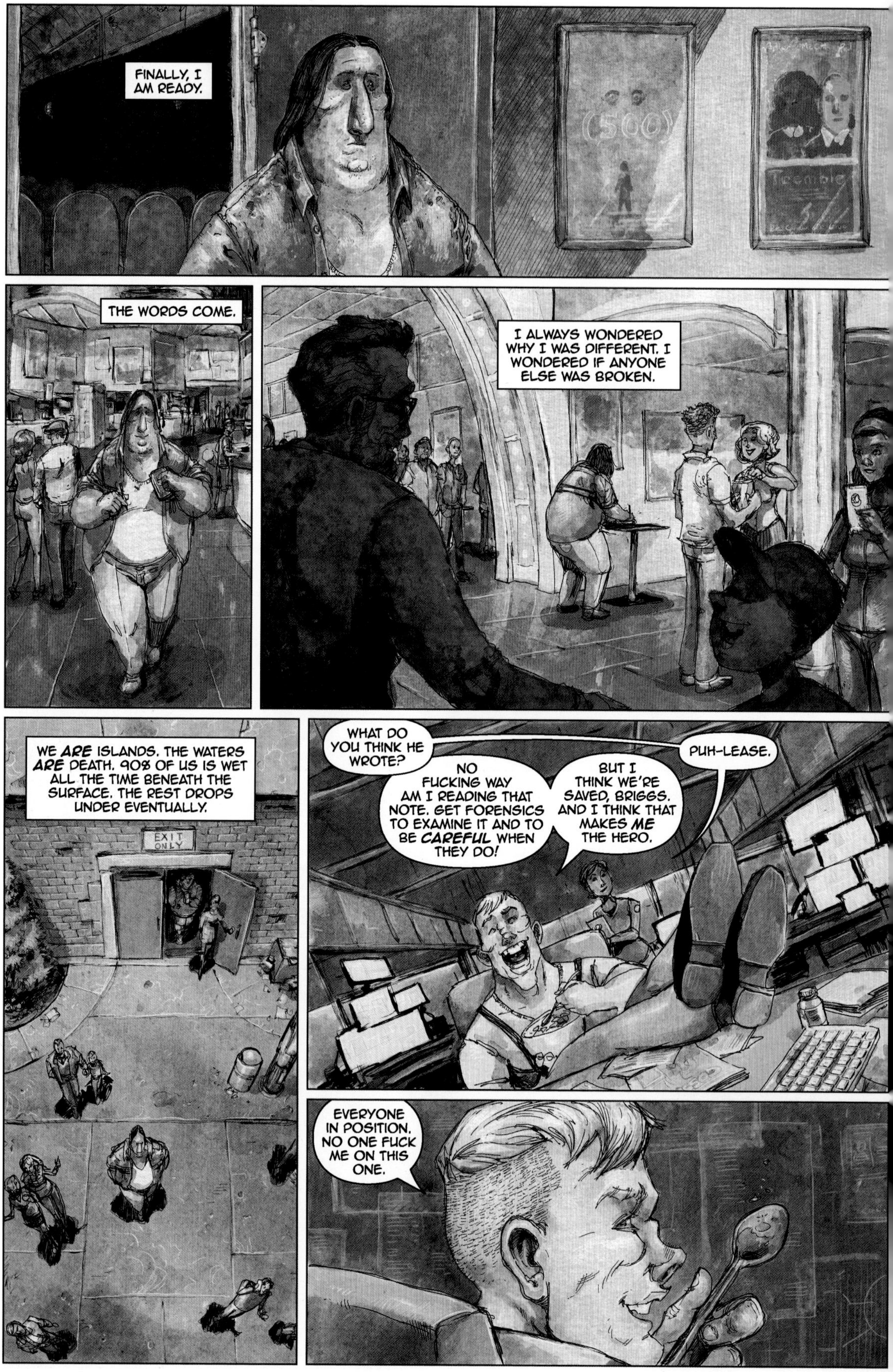
FINALLY, I AM READY.
THE WORDS COME.
I ALWAYS WONDERED WHY I WAS DIFFERENT. I WONDERED IF ANYONE ELSE WAS BROKEN.
WE ARE ISLANDS. THE WATERS ARE DEATH. 90% OF US IS WET ALL THE TIME BENEATH THE SURFACE. THE REST DROPS UNDER EVENTUALLY.
EXIT ONLY
WHAT DO YOU THINK HE WROTE?
PUH-LEASE.
NO FUCKING WAY AM I READING THAT NOTE. GET FORENSICS TO EXAMINE IT AND TO BE CAREFUL WHEN THEY DO!
BUT I THINK WE'RE SAVED, BRIGGS. AND I THINK THAT MAKES ME THE HERO.
EVERYONE IN POSITION. NO ONE FUCK ME ON THIS ONE.

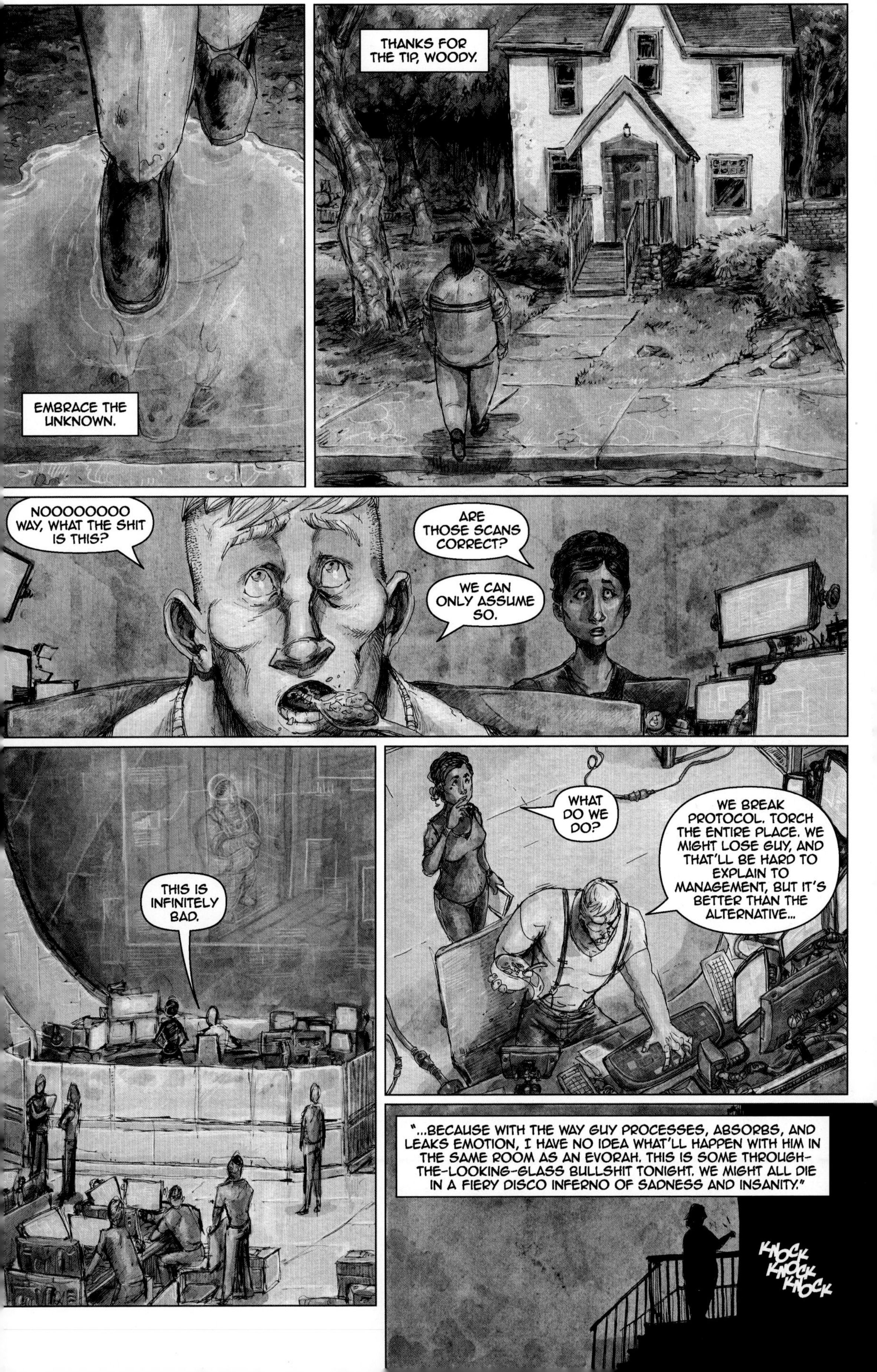
EMBRACE THE UNKNOWN.
THANKS FOR THE TIP, WOODY.
NOOOOOOOO WAY, WHAT THE SHIT IS THIS?
ARE THOSE SCANS CORRECT?
WE CAN ONLY ASSUME SO.
THIS IS INFINITELY BAD.
WHAT DO WE DO?
WE BREAK PROTOCOL. TORCH THE ENTIRE PLACE. WE MIGHT LOSE GUY, AND THAT'LL BE HARD TO EXPLAIN TO MANAGEMENT, BUT IT'S BETTER THAN THE ALTERNATIVE...
"...BECAUSE WITH THE WAY GUY PROCESSES, ABSORBS, AND LEAKS EMOTION, I HAVE NO IDEA WHAT'LL HAPPEN WITH HIM IN THE SAME ROOM AS AN EVORAH. THIS IS SOME THROUGH-THE-LOOKING-GLASS BULLSHIT TONIGHT. WE MIGHT ALL DIE IN A FIERY DISCO INFERNO OF SADNESS AND INSANITY."
KNOCK KNOCK KNOCK

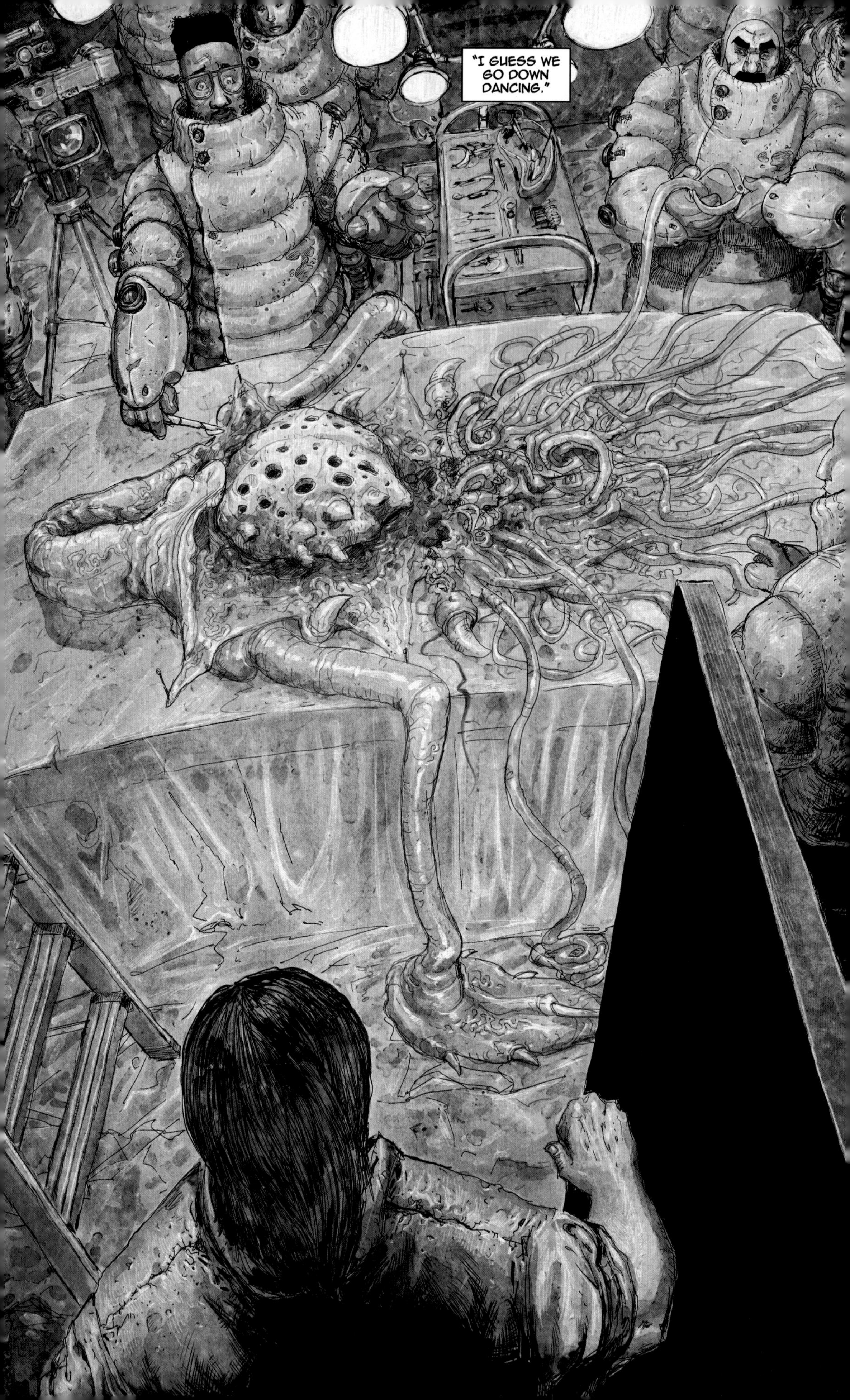
"I GUESS WE GO DOWN DANCING."

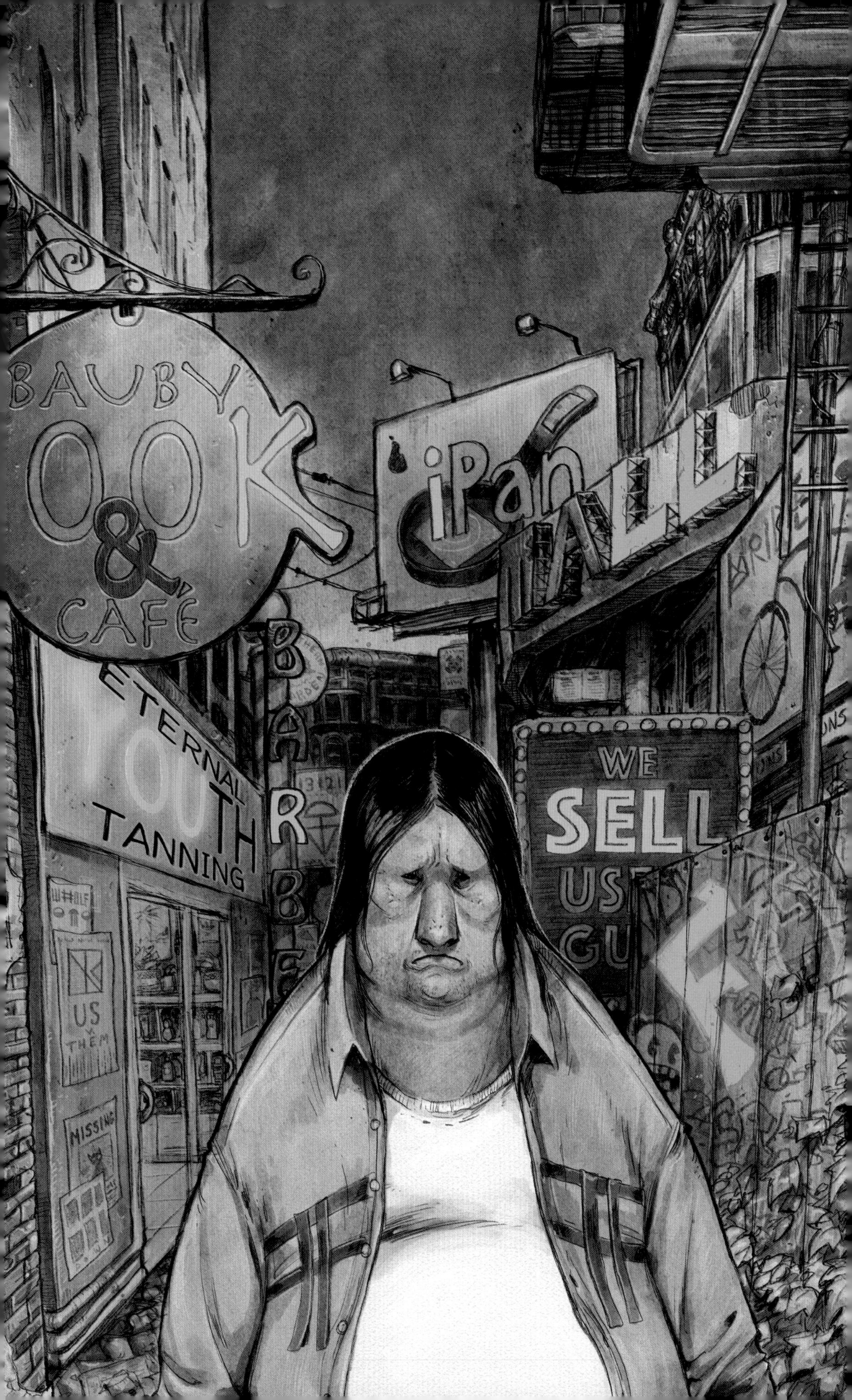

BAUBY
O & O K
CAFÉ
iPan
ETERNAL
YOUTH
TANNING
WE
SELL
US
THEM
MISSING

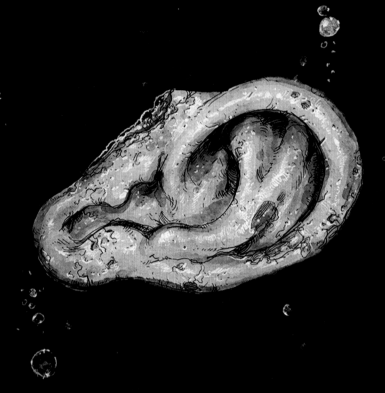

Exhibit 399

Van Gogh's Left Ear

The creatures have long taken an interest in this artist's work, procuring most of his masterpieces before they could be seen by human eyes. In the midst of one of the deepest spirals he had ever suffered, Van Gogh was told by the Evorah that if he didn't make a grand sacrifice, they would kill him. He severed his ear and delivered it to a brothel; from there it was given to the Evorah.

AD 900, GREENLAND

‹HOLD FAST!›

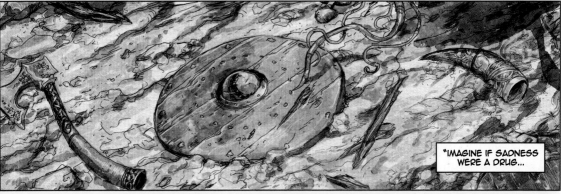

"IMAGINE IF SADNESS WERE A DRUG..."

"...AND AN ENTIRE OCEAN OF JUNKIES WERE JONESING FOR A FIX."

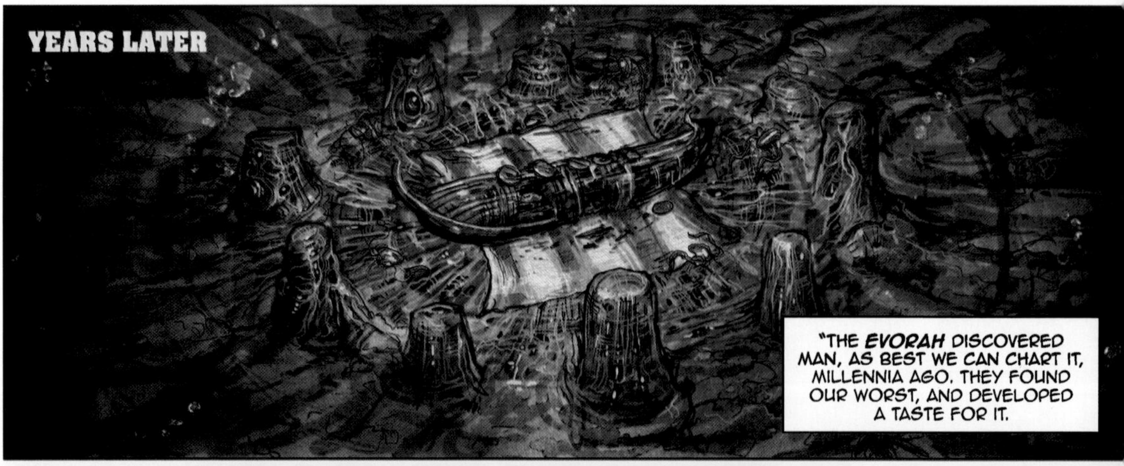
YEARS LATER
"THE EVORAH DISCOVERED MAN, AS BEST WE CAN CHART IT, MILLENNIA AGO. THEY FOUND OUR WORST, AND DEVELOPED A TASTE FOR IT.

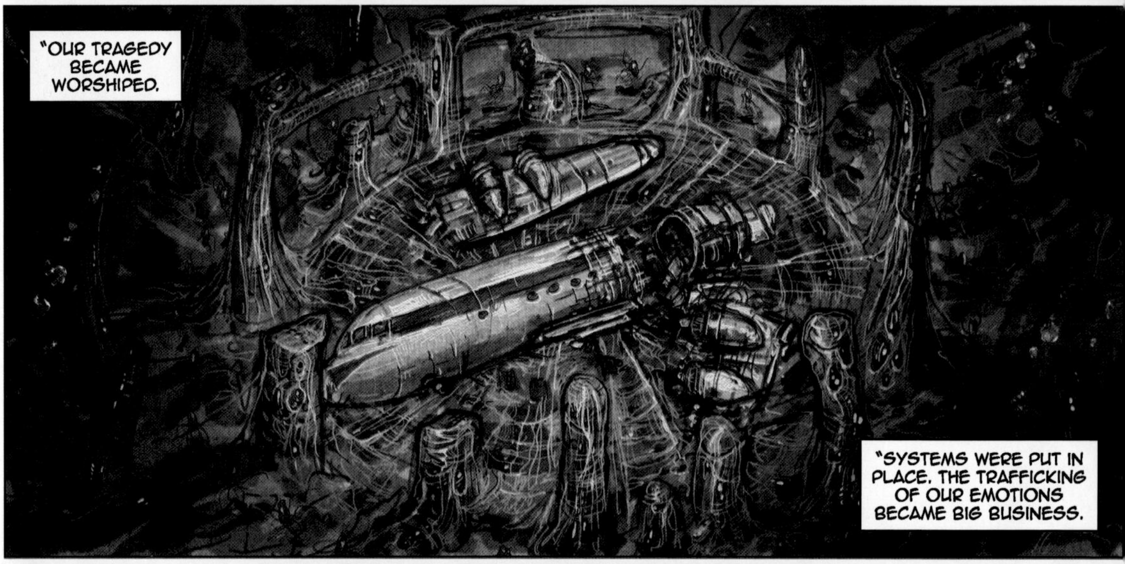
"OUR TRAGEDY BECAME WORSHIPED.
"SYSTEMS WERE PUT IN PLACE. THE TRAFFICKING OF OUR EMOTIONS BECAME BIG BUSINESS.

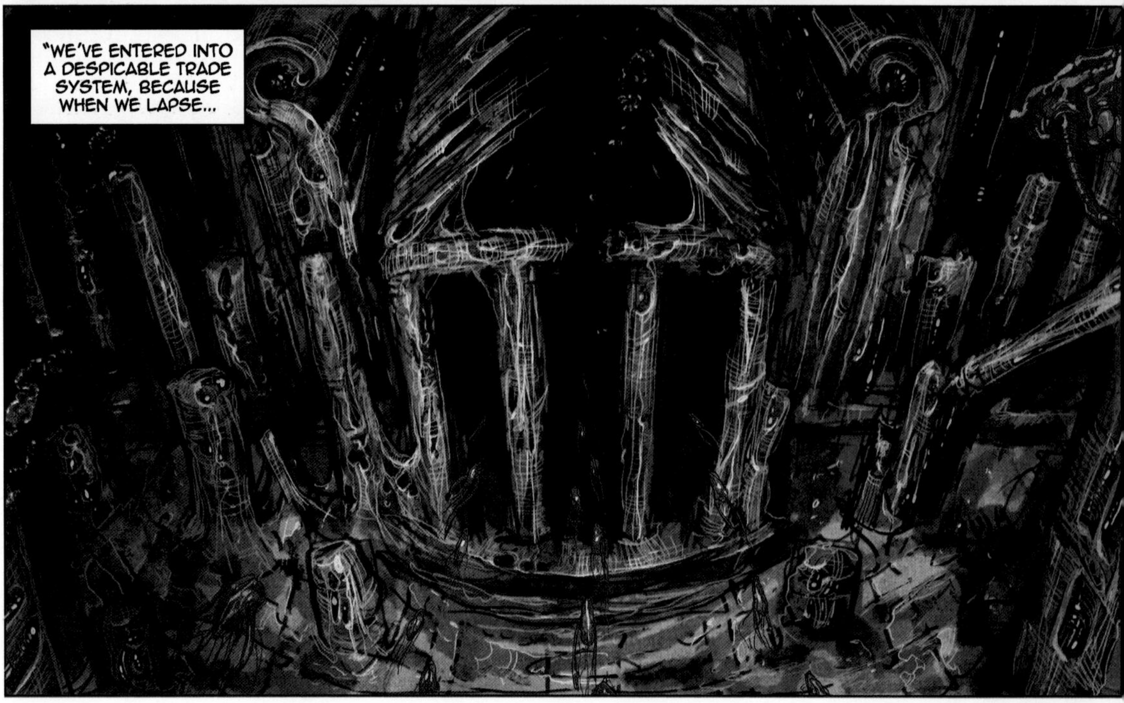
"WE'VE ENTERED INTO A DESPICABLE TRADE SYSTEM, BECAUSE WHEN WE LAPSE...

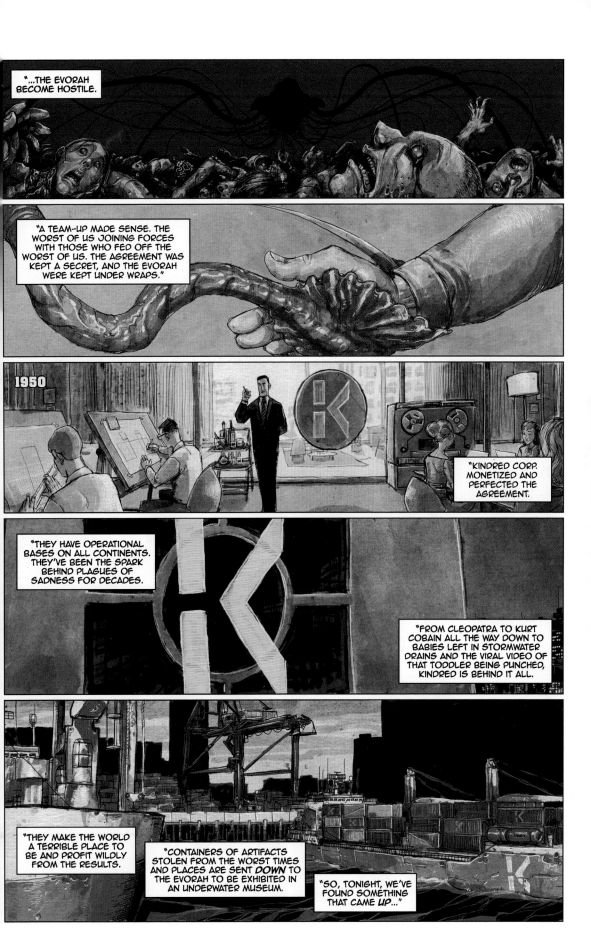

"...THE EVORAH BECOME HOSTILE.

"A TEAM-UP MADE SENSE. THE WORST OF US JOINING FORCES WITH THOSE WHO FED OFF THE WORST OF US. THE AGREEMENT WAS KEPT A SECRET, AND THE EVORAH WERE KEPT UNDER WRAPS."

1950

"KINDRED CORP. MONETIZED AND PERFECTED THE AGREEMENT.

"THEY HAVE OPERATIONAL BASES ON ALL CONTINENTS. THEY'VE BEEN THE SPARK BEHIND PLAGUES OF SADNESS FOR DECADES.

"FROM CLEOPATRA TO KURT COBAIN ALL THE WAY DOWN TO BABIES LEFT IN STORMWATER DRAINS AND THE VIRAL VIDEO OF THAT TODDLER BEING PUNCHED, KINDRED IS BEHIND IT ALL.

"THEY MAKE THE WORLD A TERRIBLE PLACE TO BE AND PROFIT WILDLY FROM THE RESULTS.

"CONTAINERS OF ARTIFACTS STOLEN FROM THE WORST TIMES AND PLACES ARE SENT *DOWN* TO THE EVORAH TO BE EXHIBITED IN AN UNDERWATER MUSEUM.

"SO, TONIGHT, WE'VE FOUND SOMETHING THAT CAME *UP*..."

...AND WE'VE NOW STOLEN IT FROM THEM IN ORDER TO MAKE US ALL INCREDIBLY HAPPY.

KINDRED CALL US *STRANGERS*. IT FITS. WE'RE ALL A LITTLE STR--

WHO ARE *YOU?*

I'M THE GUY FIGHTING THE GOOD FIGHT. INSTEAD OF BEING MANIPULATED, PUSHED, MOLDED, WE ARE GOING TO BRING DOWN KINDRED AND RETURN TO A BALANCE AND NORMALCY WE HAVEN'T FELT FOR DECADES.

AN EMOTIONAL PLAYING FIELD OUR GENERATION DOESN'T EVEN KNOW EXISTS, GUY.

YOU'RE GOING TO FIGHT A WAR AGAINST--WHAT, *BAD FEELINGS?*

EXACTLY! AND WE'LL HAVE THE ONLY WEAPON THAT MATTERS--GOOD FEELINGS.

TONIGHT WE'VE *FINALLY* FOUND IT.

WE'VE BEEN PIECING OUR PLAN TOGETHER FOR A LONG TIME NOW. WE'VE GOT THE NUMBERS, THE KNOWLEDGE, THE TINY DETAILS, THE MUSCLE, AND NOW...

...NOW WE'VE GOT THE *BRAINS.*

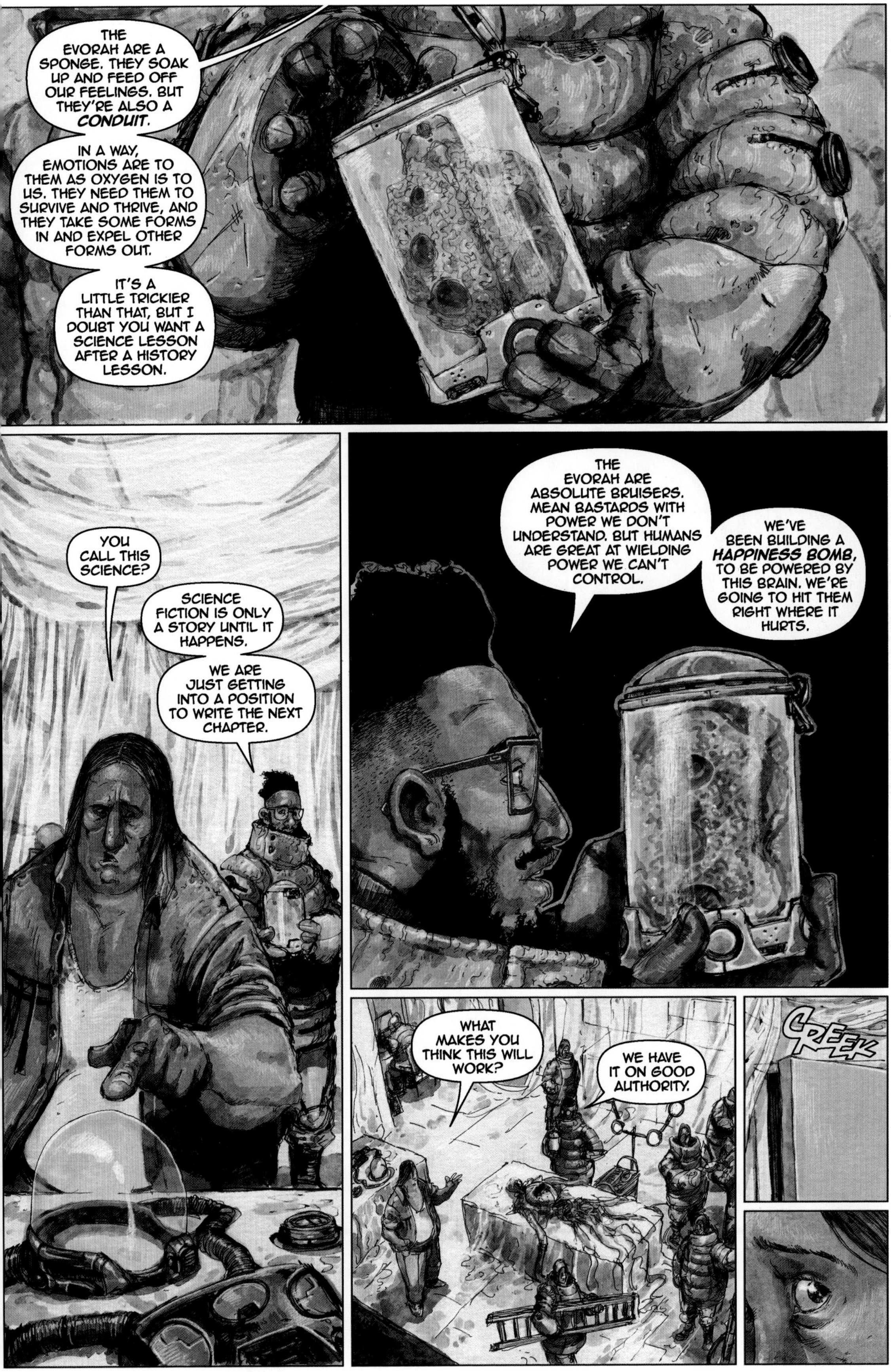
THE EVORAH ARE A SPONGE. THEY SOAK UP AND FEED OFF OUR FEELINGS. BUT THEY'RE ALSO A *CONDUIT*.
IN A WAY, EMOTIONS ARE TO THEM AS OXYGEN IS TO US. THEY NEED THEM TO SURVIVE AND THRIVE, AND THEY TAKE SOME FORMS IN AND EXPEL OTHER FORMS OUT.
IT'S A LITTLE TRICKIER THAN THAT, BUT I DOUBT YOU WANT A SCIENCE LESSON AFTER A HISTORY LESSON.
YOU CALL THIS SCIENCE?
SCIENCE FICTION IS ONLY A STORY UNTIL IT HAPPENS.
WE ARE JUST GETTING INTO A POSITION TO WRITE THE NEXT CHAPTER.
THE EVORAH ARE ABSOLUTE BRUISERS. MEAN BASTARDS WITH POWER WE DON'T UNDERSTAND. BUT HUMANS ARE GREAT AT WIELDING POWER WE CAN'T CONTROL.
WE'VE BEEN BUILDING A *HAPPINESS BOMB*, TO BE POWERED BY THIS BRAIN. WE'RE GOING TO HIT THEM RIGHT WHERE IT HURTS.
WHAT MAKES YOU THINK THIS WILL WORK?
WE HAVE IT ON GOOD AUTHORITY.
CREEK

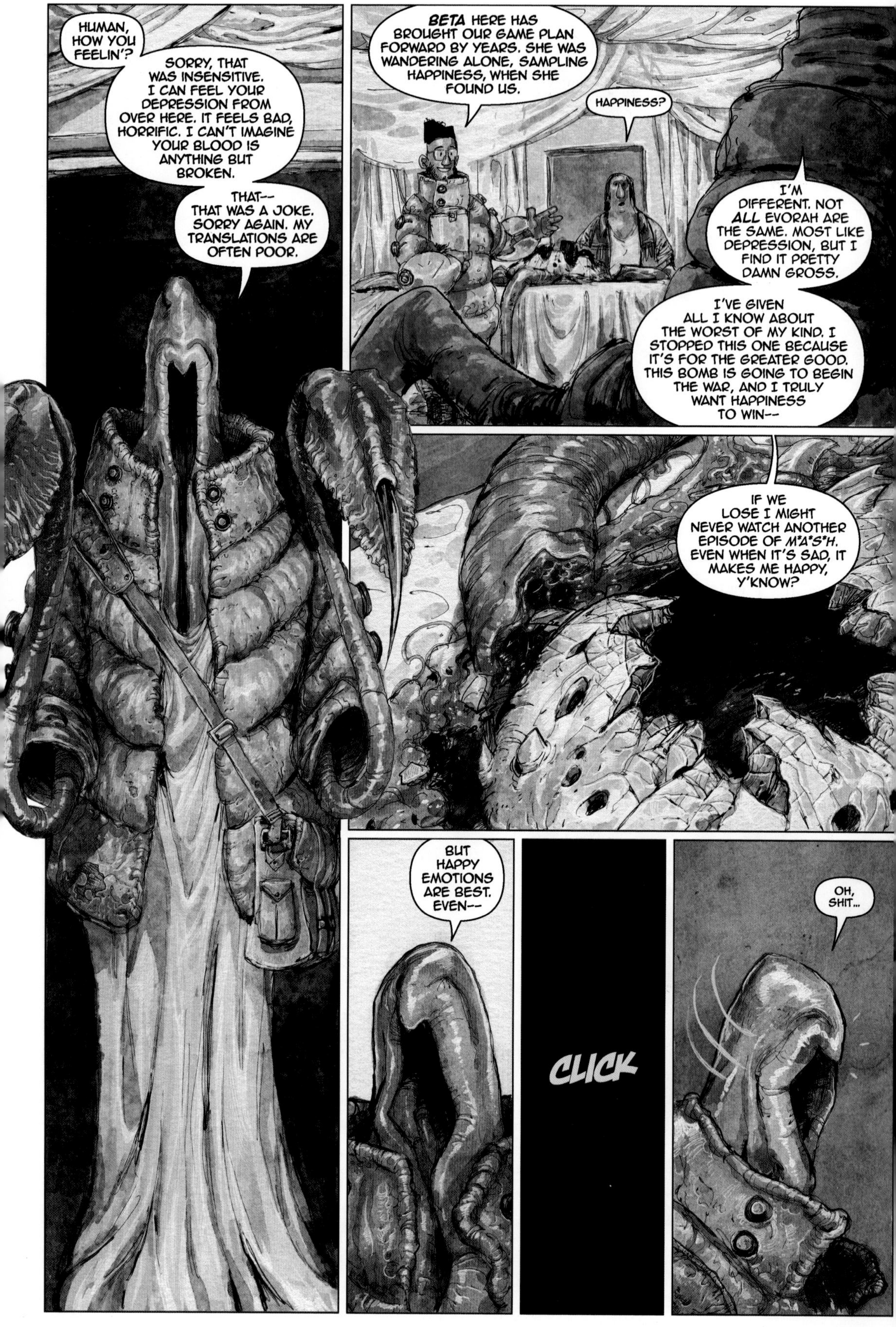
HUMAN, HOW YOU FEELIN'?
SORRY, THAT WAS INSENSITIVE. I CAN FEEL YOUR DEPRESSION FROM OVER HERE. IT FEELS BAD, HORRIFIC. I CAN'T IMAGINE YOUR BLOOD IS ANYTHING BUT BROKEN.
THAT-- THAT WAS A JOKE. SORRY AGAIN. MY TRANSLATIONS ARE OFTEN POOR.
BETA HERE HAS BROUGHT OUR GAME PLAN FORWARD BY YEARS. SHE WAS WANDERING ALONE, SAMPLING HAPPINESS, WHEN SHE FOUND US.
HAPPINESS?
I'M DIFFERENT. NOT ALL EVORAH ARE THE SAME. MOST LIKE DEPRESSION, BUT I FIND IT PRETTY DAMN GROSS.
I'VE GIVEN ALL I KNOW ABOUT THE WORST OF MY KIND. I STOPPED THIS ONE BECAUSE IT'S FOR THE GREATER GOOD. THIS BOMB IS GOING TO BEGIN THE WAR, AND I TRULY WANT HAPPINESS TO WIN--
IF WE LOSE I MIGHT NEVER WATCH ANOTHER EPISODE OF M*A*S*H. EVEN WHEN IT'S SAD, IT MAKES ME HAPPY, Y'KNOW?
BUT HAPPY EMOTIONS ARE BEST. EVEN--
CLICK
OH, SHIT...

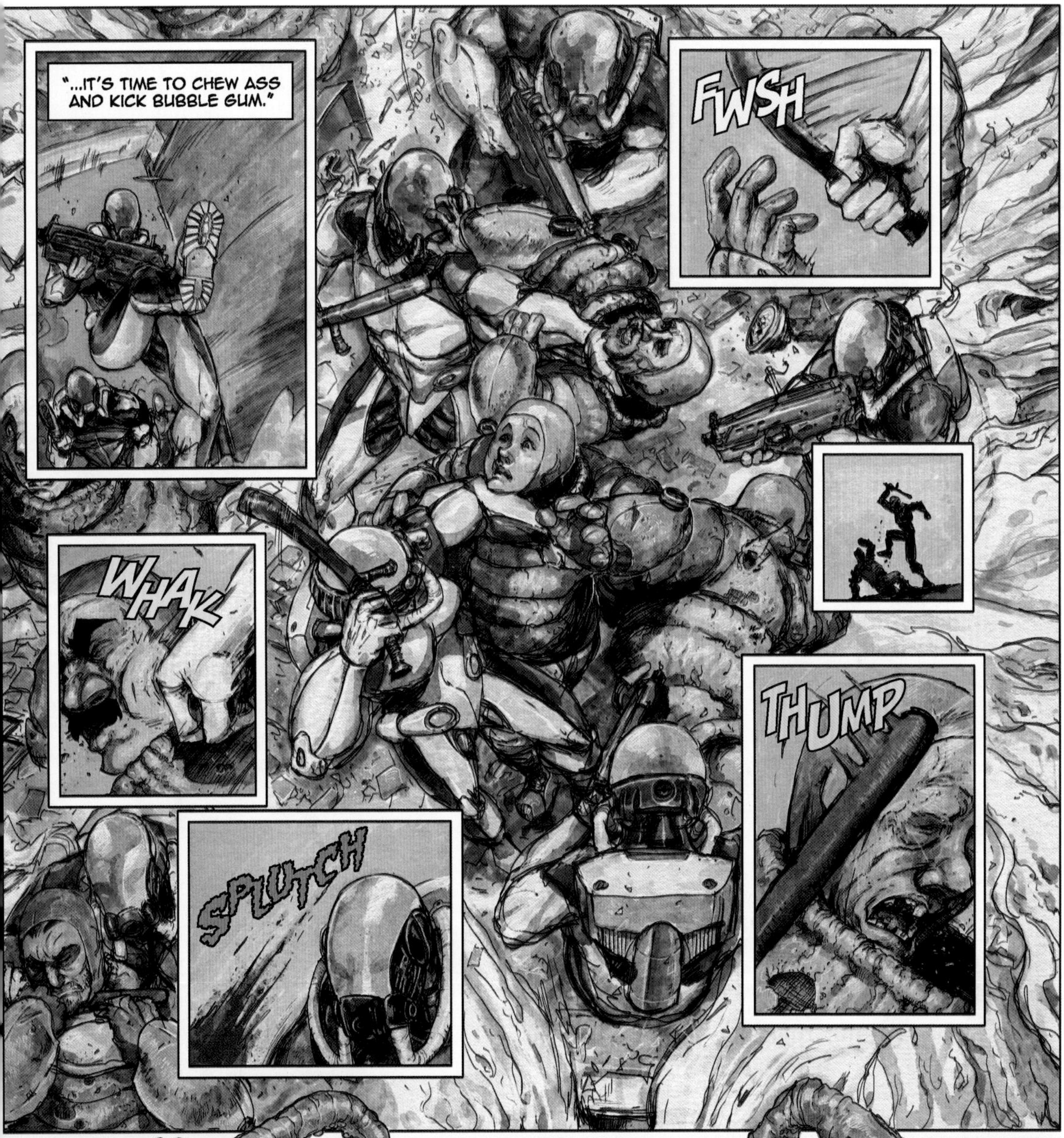
"...IT'S TIME TO CHEW ASS AND KICK BUBBLE GUM."
FWSH
WHAK
THUMP
SPLUTCH

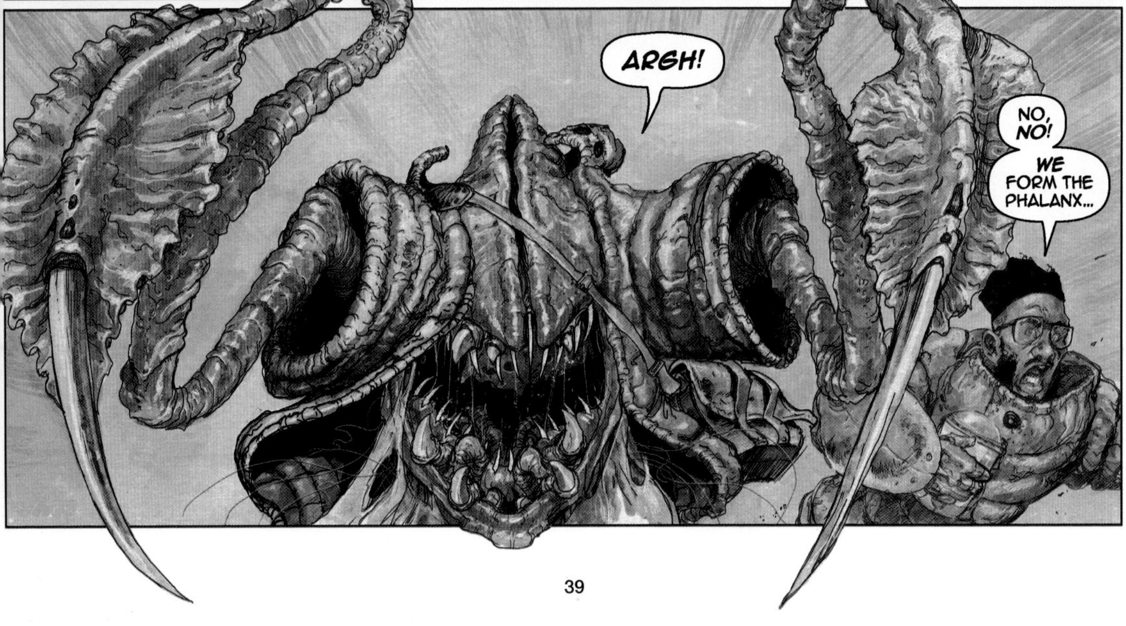
ARGH!
NO, NO! WE FORM THE PHALANX...

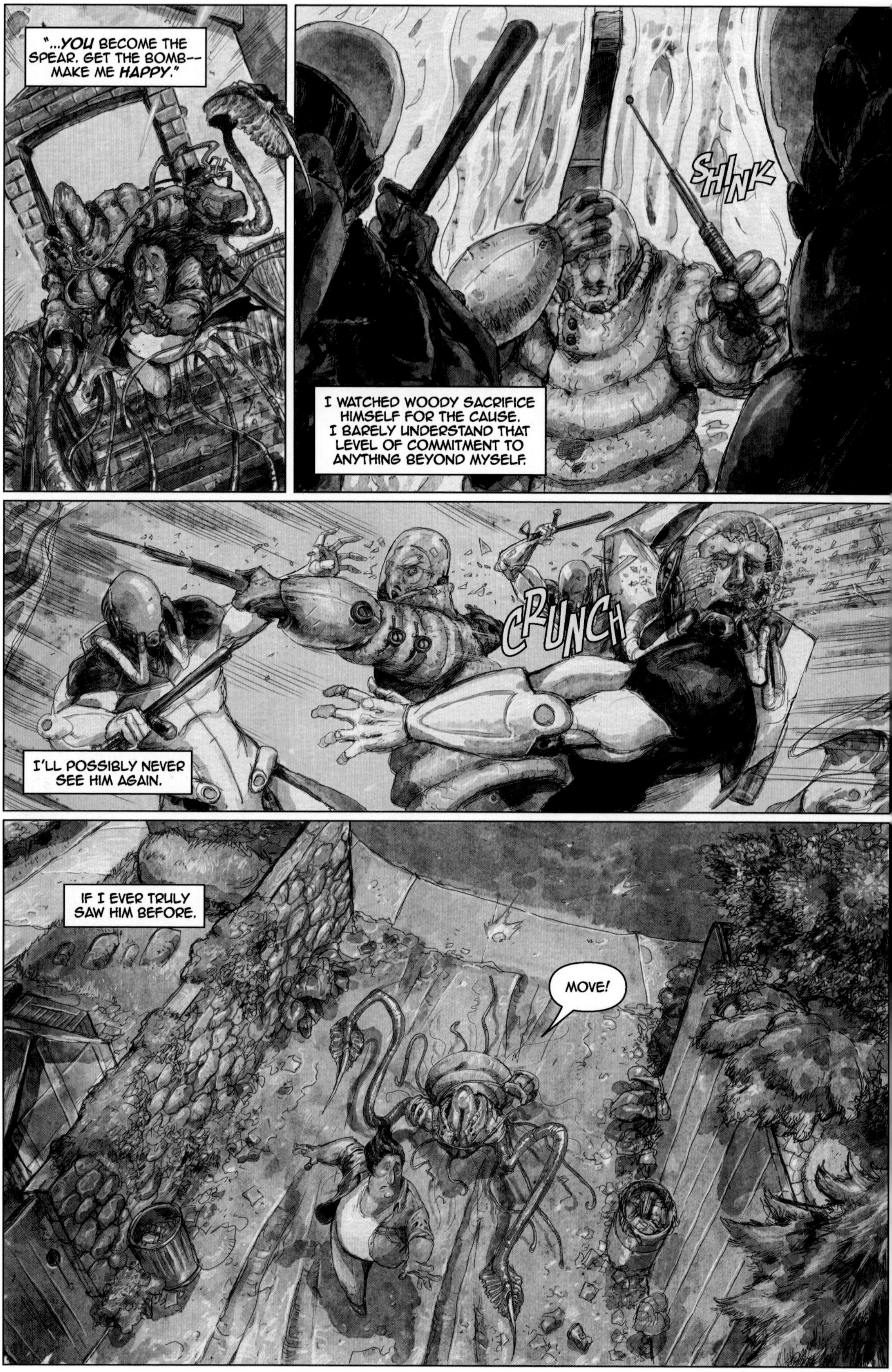
"...YOU BECOME THE SPEAR. GET THE BOMB-- MAKE ME HAPPY."
SHINK
I WATCHED WOODY SACRIFICE HIMSELF FOR THE CAUSE. I BARELY UNDERSTAND THAT LEVEL OF COMMITMENT TO ANYTHING BEYOND MYSELF.
CRUNCH
I'LL POSSIBLY NEVER SEE HIM AGAIN.
IF I EVER TRULY SAW HIM BEFORE.
MOVE!

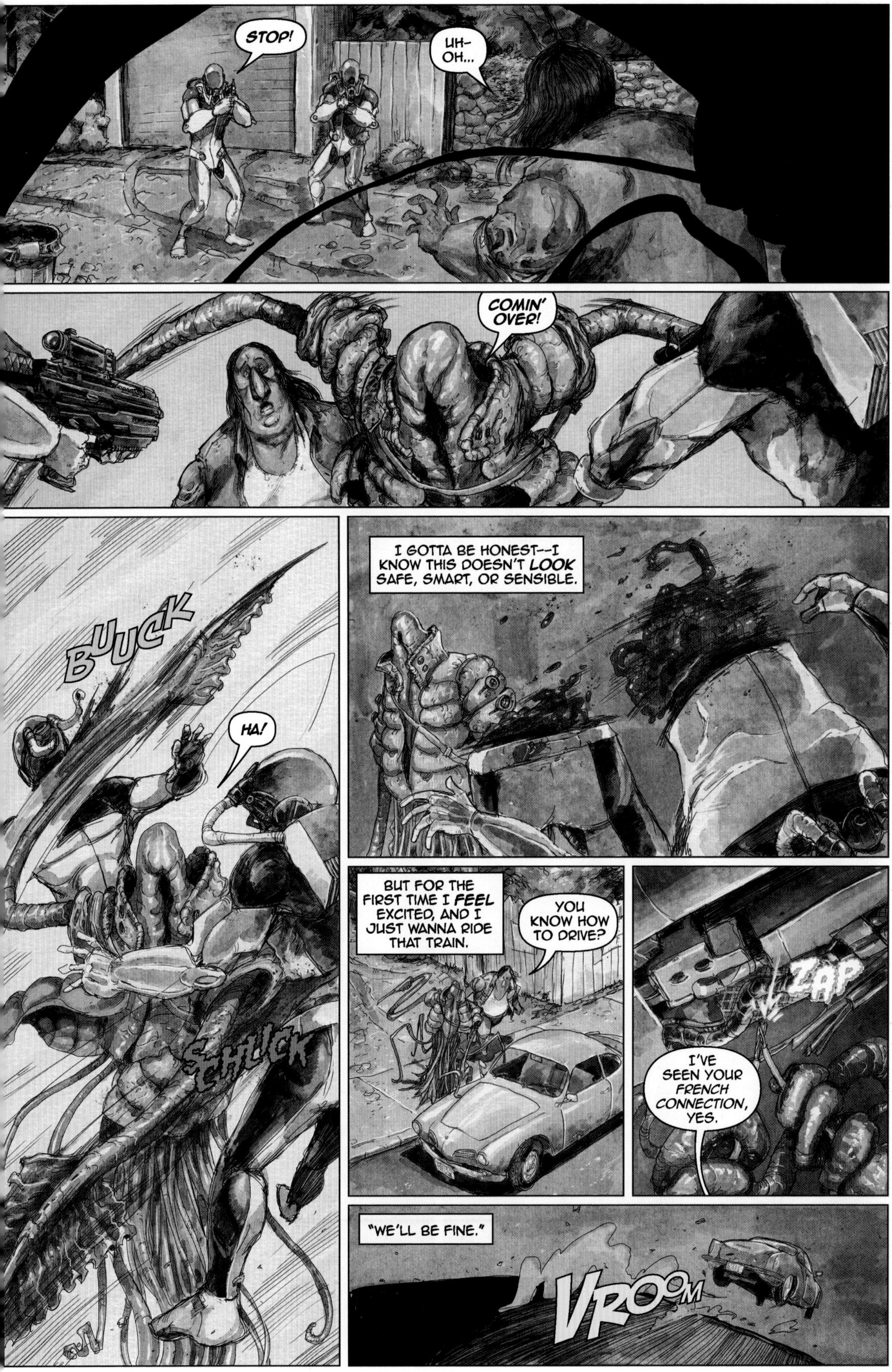
STOP!
UH-OH...
COMIN' OVER!
BUUCK
HA!
CHUCK
I GOTTA BE HONEST--I KNOW THIS DOESN'T **LOOK** SAFE, SMART, OR SENSIBLE.
BUT FOR THE FIRST TIME I **FEEL** EXCITED, AND I JUST WANNA RIDE THAT TRAIN.
YOU KNOW HOW TO DRIVE?
ZAP
I'VE SEEN YOUR FRENCH CONNECTION, YES.
"WE'LL BE FINE."
VROOM

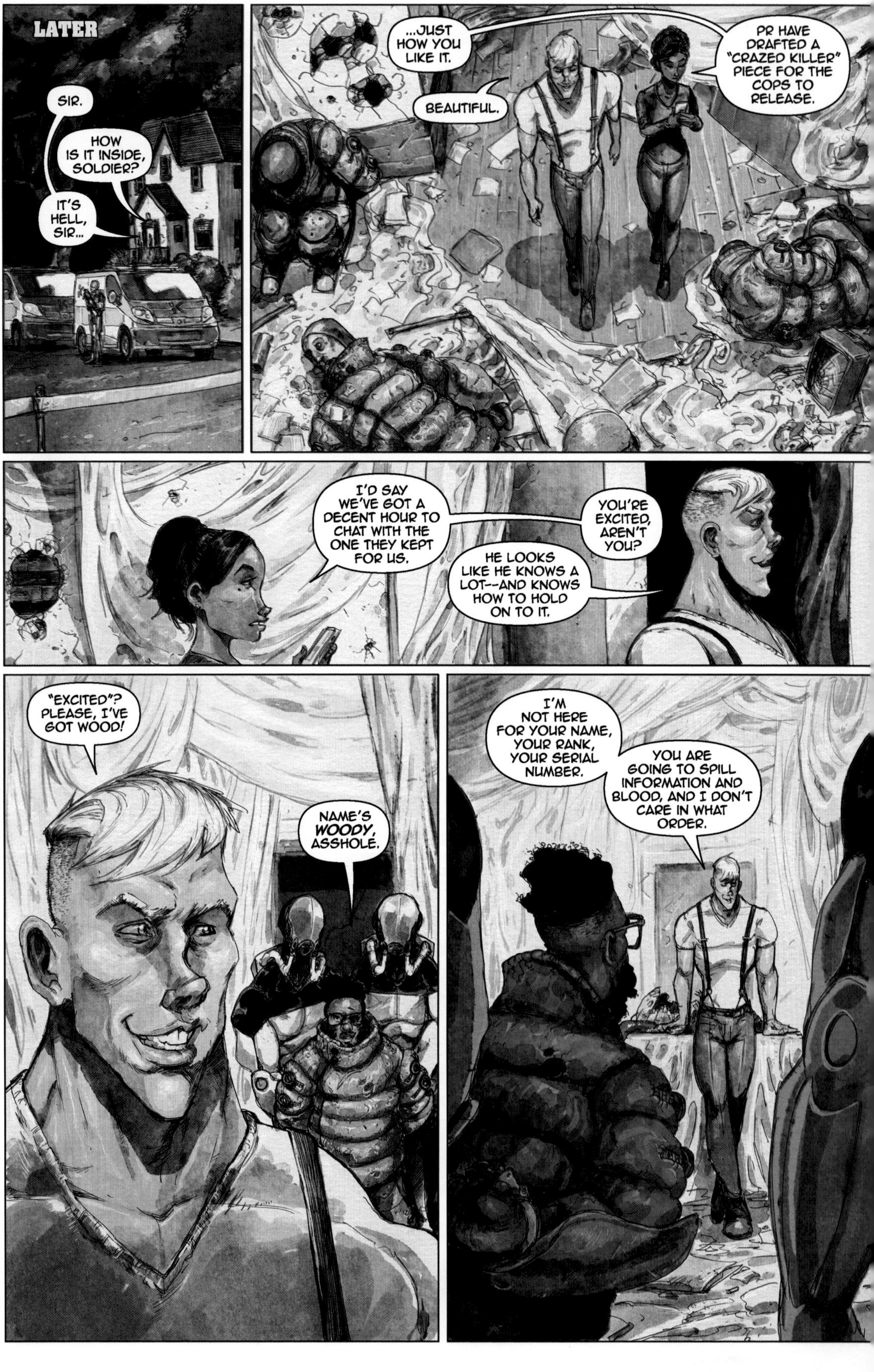
LATER
SIR.
HOW IS IT INSIDE, SOLDIER?
IT'S HELL, SIR...
...JUST HOW YOU LIKE IT.
PR HAVE DRAFTED A "CRAZED KILLER" PIECE FOR THE COPS TO RELEASE.
BEAUTIFUL.
I'D SAY WE'VE GOT A DECENT HOUR TO CHAT WITH THE ONE THEY KEPT FOR US.
YOU'RE EXCITED, AREN'T YOU?
HE LOOKS LIKE HE KNOWS A LOT--AND KNOWS HOW TO HOLD ON TO IT.
"EXCITED"? PLEASE, I'VE GOT WOOD!
NAME'S WOODY, ASSHOLE.
I'M NOT HERE FOR YOUR NAME, YOUR RANK, YOUR SERIAL NUMBER.
YOU ARE GOING TO SPILL INFORMATION AND BLOOD, AND I DON'T CARE IN WHAT ORDER.

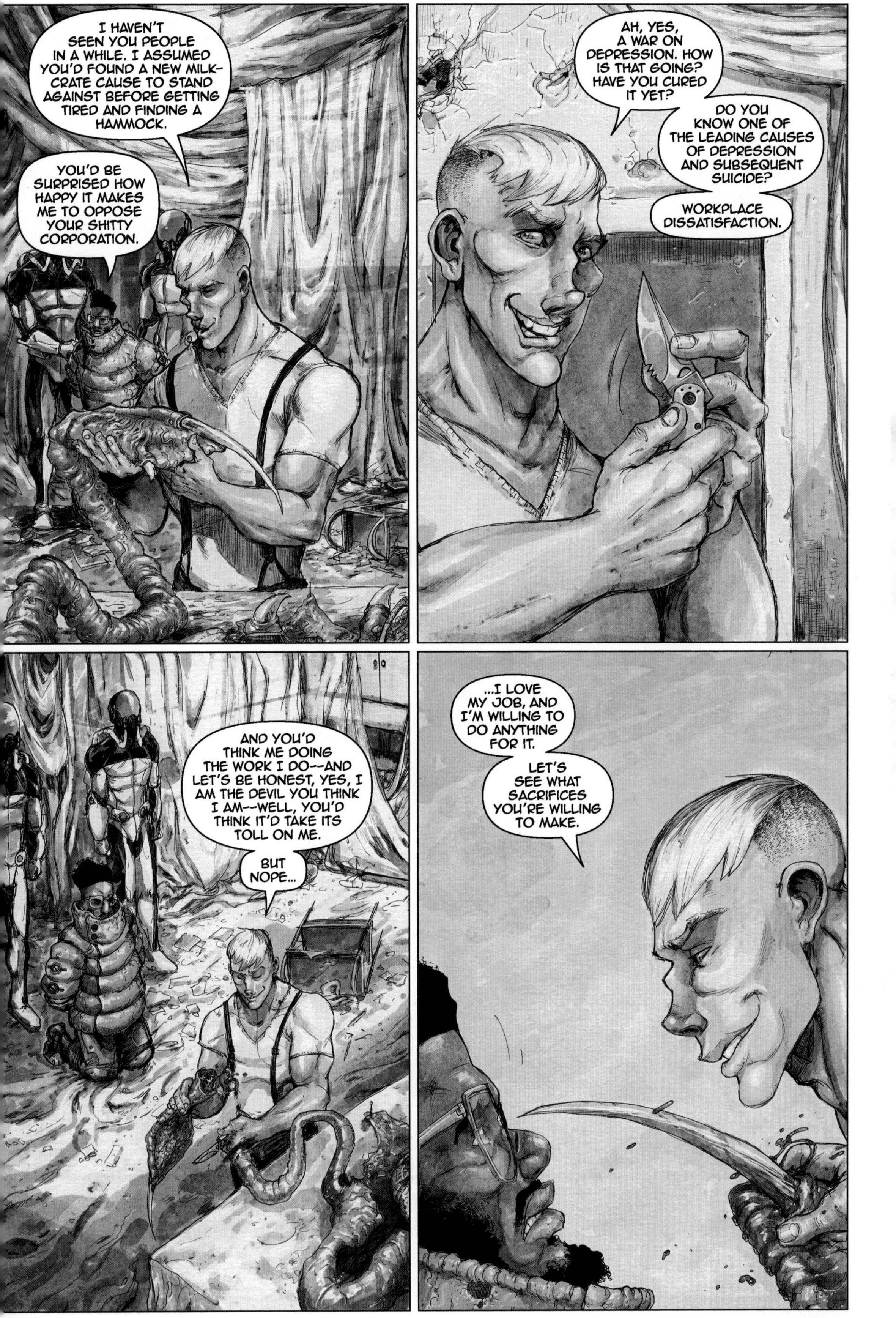
I HAVEN'T SEEN YOU PEOPLE IN A WHILE. I ASSUMED YOU'D FOUND A NEW MILK-CRATE CAUSE TO STAND AGAINST BEFORE GETTING TIRED AND FINDING A HAMMOCK.
YOU'D BE SURPRISED HOW HAPPY IT MAKES ME TO OPPOSE YOUR SHITTY CORPORATION.
AH, YES, A WAR ON DEPRESSION. HOW IS THAT GOING? HAVE YOU CURED IT YET?
DO YOU KNOW ONE OF THE LEADING CAUSES OF DEPRESSION AND SUBSEQUENT SUICIDE?
WORKPLACE DISSATISFACTION.
AND YOU'D THINK ME DOING THE WORK I DO--AND LET'S BE HONEST, YES, I AM THE DEVIL YOU THINK I AM--WELL, YOU'D THINK IT'D TAKE ITS TOLL ON ME.
BUT NOPE...
...I LOVE MY JOB, AND I'M WILLING TO DO ANYTHING FOR IT.
LET'S SEE WHAT SACRIFICES YOU'RE WILLING TO MAKE.

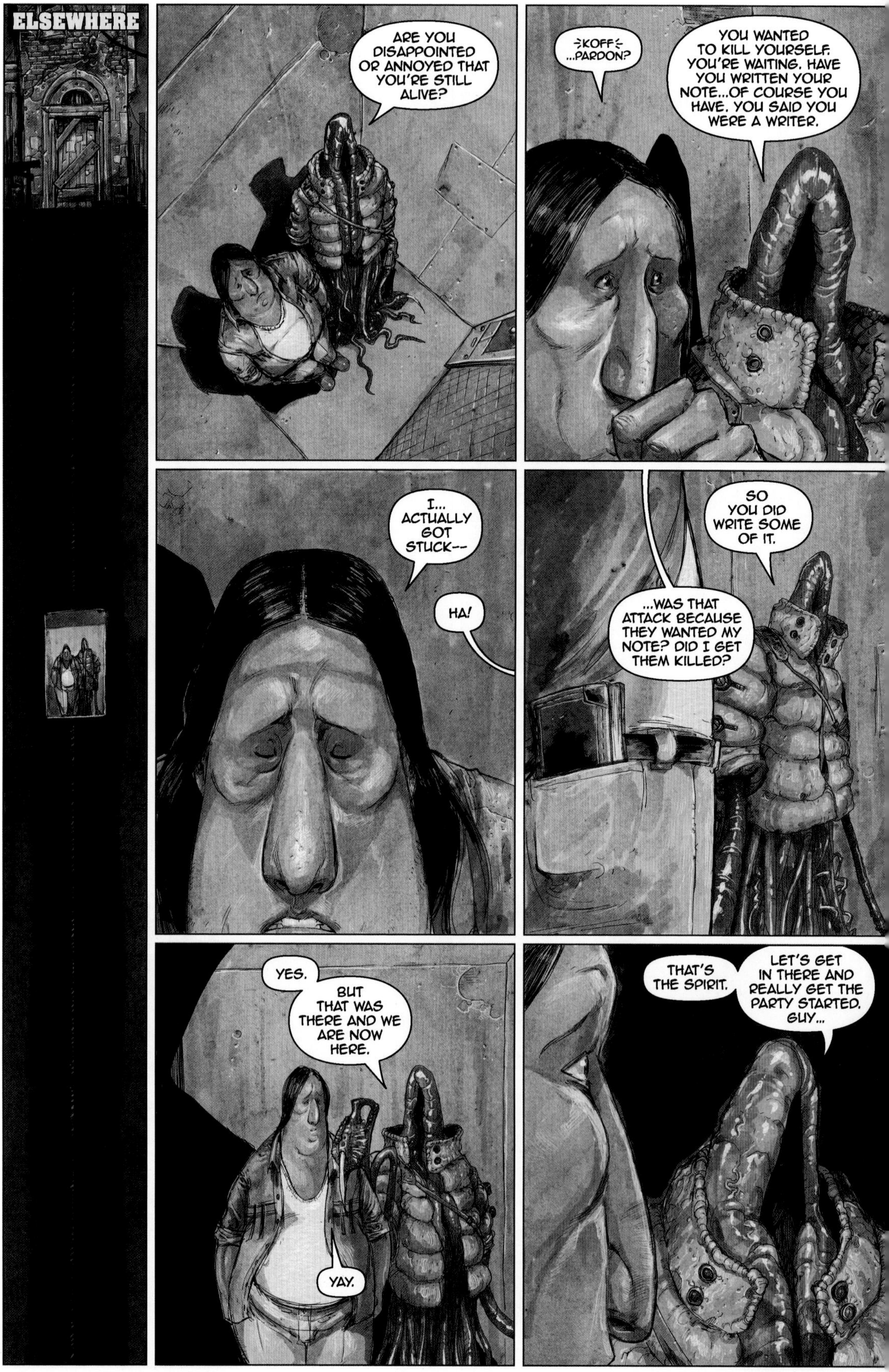
ELSEWHERE
ARE YOU DISAPPOINTED OR ANNOYED THAT YOU'RE STILL ALIVE?
KOFF ...PARDON?
YOU WANTED TO KILL YOURSELF. YOU'RE WAITING. HAVE YOU WRITTEN YOUR NOTE...OF COURSE YOU HAVE. YOU SAID YOU WERE A WRITER.
I... ACTUALLY GOT STUCK--
HA!
SO YOU DID WRITE SOME OF IT.
...WAS THAT ATTACK BECAUSE THEY WANTED MY NOTE? DID I GET THEM KILLED?
YES.
BUT THAT WAS THERE AND WE ARE NOW HERE.
YAY.
THAT'S THE SPIRIT.
LET'S GET IN THERE AND REALLY GET THE PARTY STARTED, GUY...

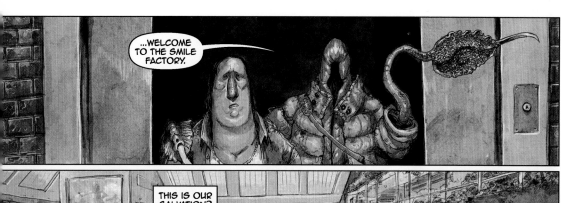

...WELCOME TO THE SMILE FACTORY.

THIS IS OUR SALVATION?

CAN'T THEY SHOW SOME RESPECT FOR THE REST OF US NORMAL, UNHAPPY PEOPLE?

WE'VE BEEN FIGHTING THE GOOD FIGHT FOR A LONG TIME. GUERRILLA HAPPINESS ONE COFFEE OR OLD BOOK OR RANDOM SMILE AT A TIME.

KINDRED NEVER KNOW HOW TO FIND OR STOP US BECAUSE OUR WEAPONS ARE SUBTLE, OUR MEANS ARE VIRAL.

BUT NOW WE CAN LEVEL UP.

FRANNIE, CAN YOU TELL GEORGINA TO GET ME THE H-BOMB RIGHT NOW, PLEASE?

NO PROBLEM, BETA!

THE PLAN IS EASY. WE DESTROY THE EVORAH MUSEUM OF SADNESS WITH A HAPPINESS BOMB. WE--I'M PULLING A SLIGHT AUDIBLE--

WAIT... WAAAAIIIT, WHAT THE F--

!

KAFUKU SOUP BAR

GUESS WE DO THIS NOW THEN.

45

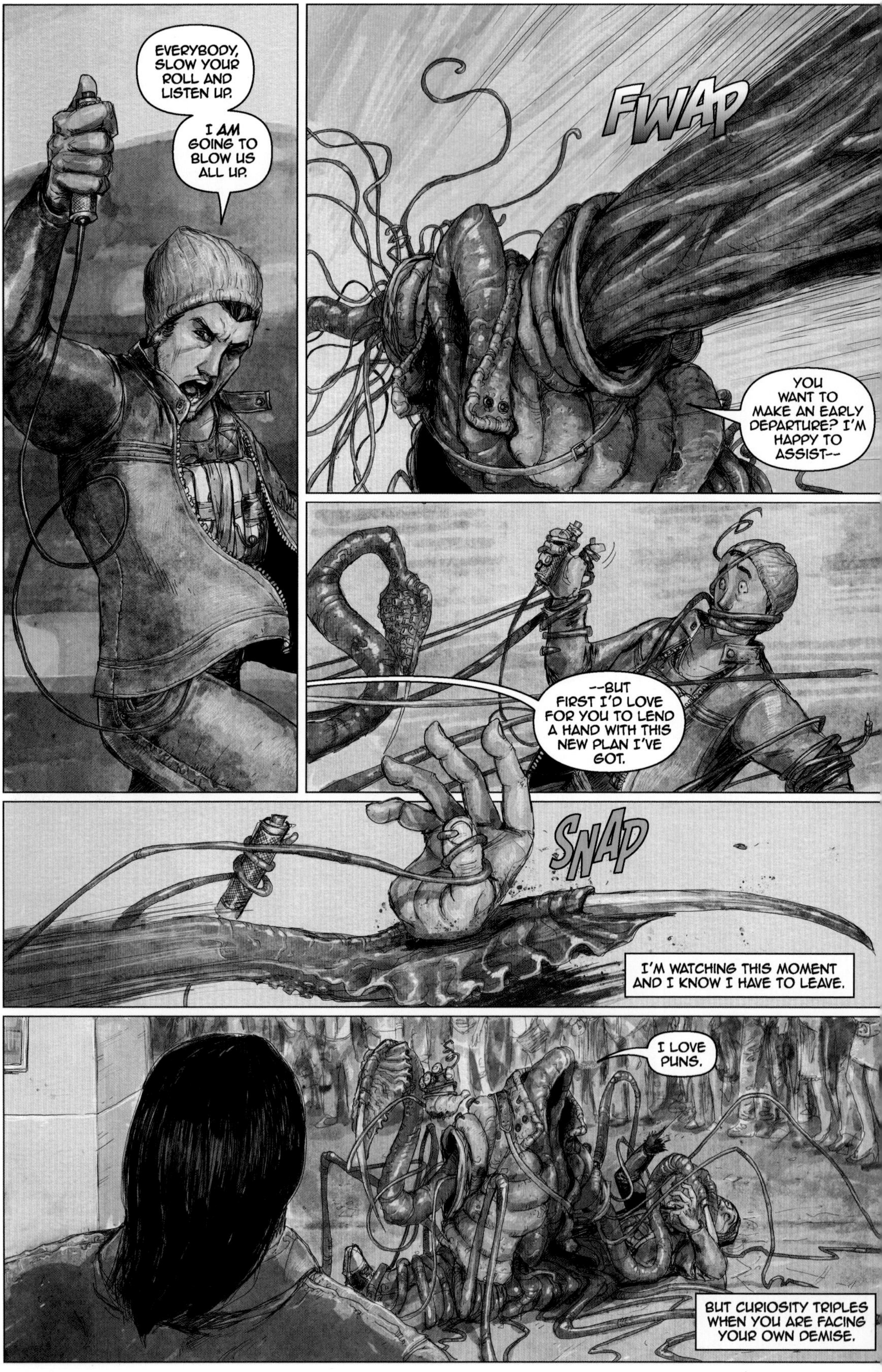
EVERYBODY, SLOW YOUR ROLL AND LISTEN UP.
I AM GOING TO BLOW US ALL UP.
FWAP
YOU WANT TO MAKE AN EARLY DEPARTURE? I'M HAPPY TO ASSIST--
--BUT FIRST I'D LOVE FOR YOU TO LEND A HAND WITH THIS NEW PLAN I'VE GOT.
SNAP
I'M WATCHING THIS MOMENT AND I KNOW I HAVE TO LEAVE.
I LOVE PUNS.
BUT CURIOSITY TRIPLES WHEN YOU ARE FACING YOUR OWN DEMISE.

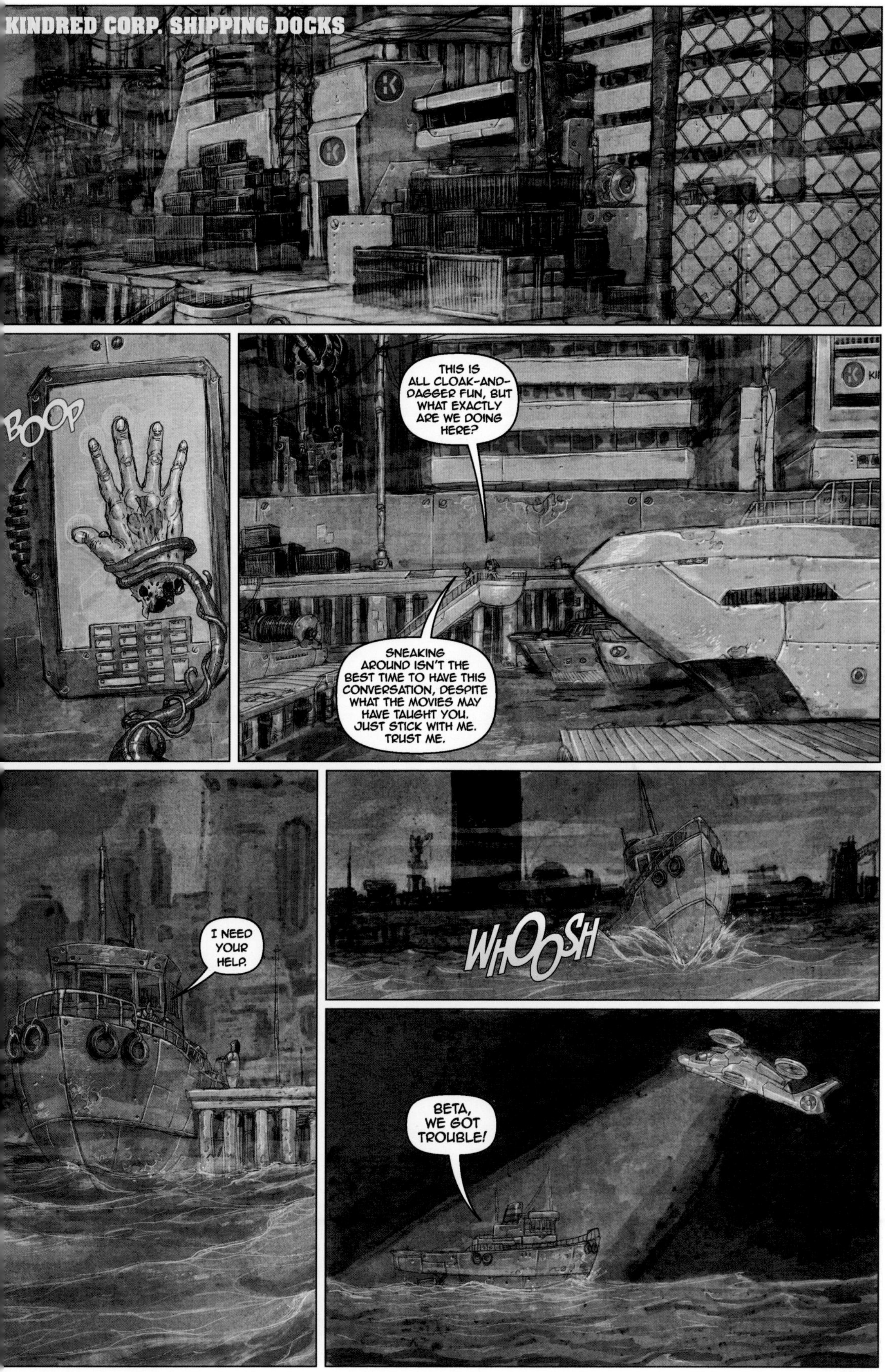
KINDRED CORP. SHIPPING DOCKS
BOOP
THIS IS ALL CLOAK-AND-DAGGER FUN, BUT WHAT EXACTLY ARE WE DOING HERE?
SNEAKING AROUND ISN'T THE BEST TIME TO HAVE THIS CONVERSATION, DESPITE WHAT THE MOVIES MAY HAVE TAUGHT YOU. JUST STICK WITH ME. TRUST ME.
I NEED YOUR HELP.
WHOOSH
BETA, WE GOT TROUBLE!

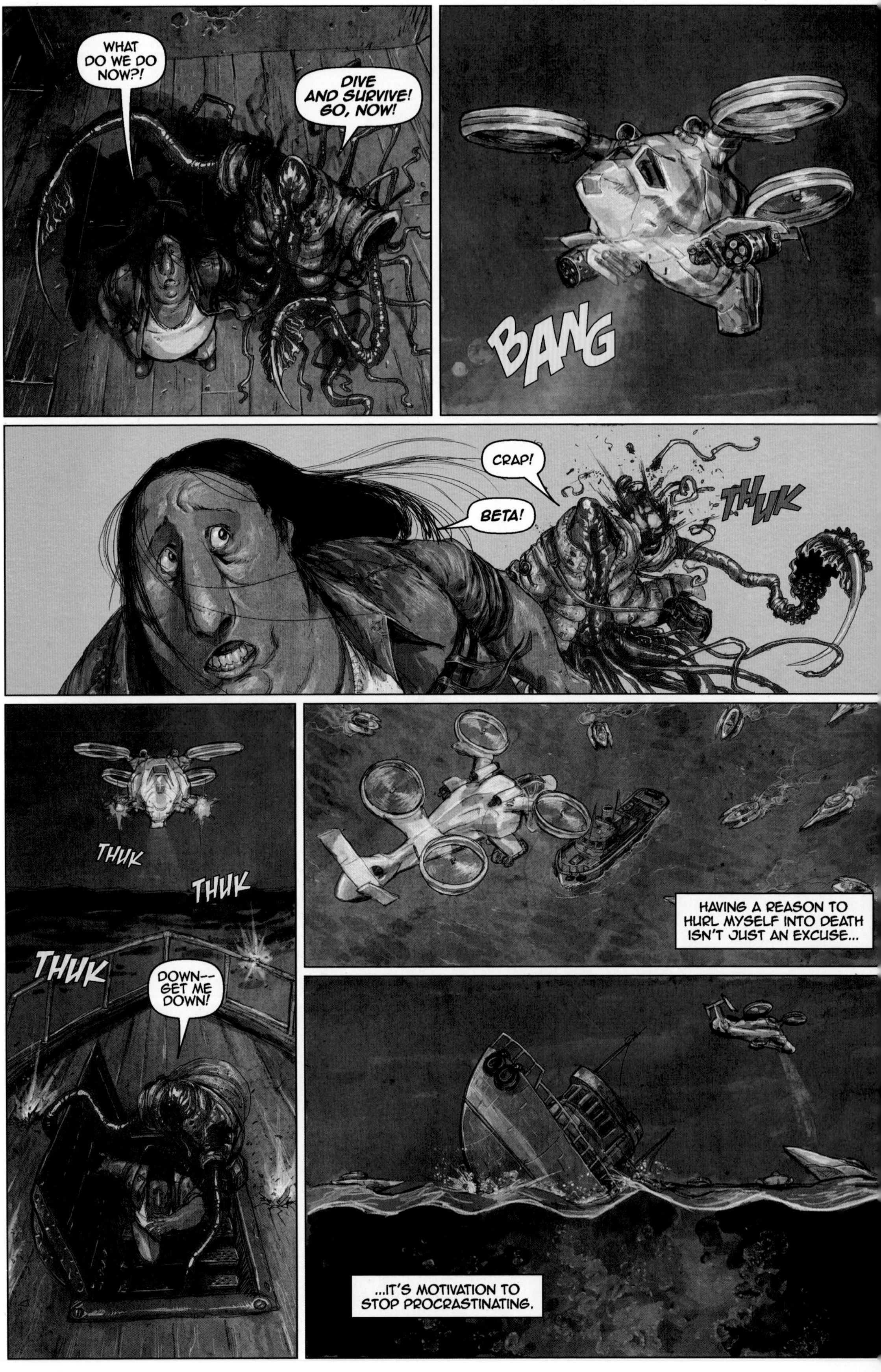
WHAT DO WE DO NOW?!
DIVE AND SURVIVE! GO, NOW!
BANG
CRAP!
BETA!
THUK
THUK
THUK
THUK
DOWN-- GET ME DOWN!
HAVING A REASON TO HURL MYSELF INTO DEATH ISN'T JUST AN EXCUSE...
...IT'S MOTIVATION TO STOP PROCRASTINATING.

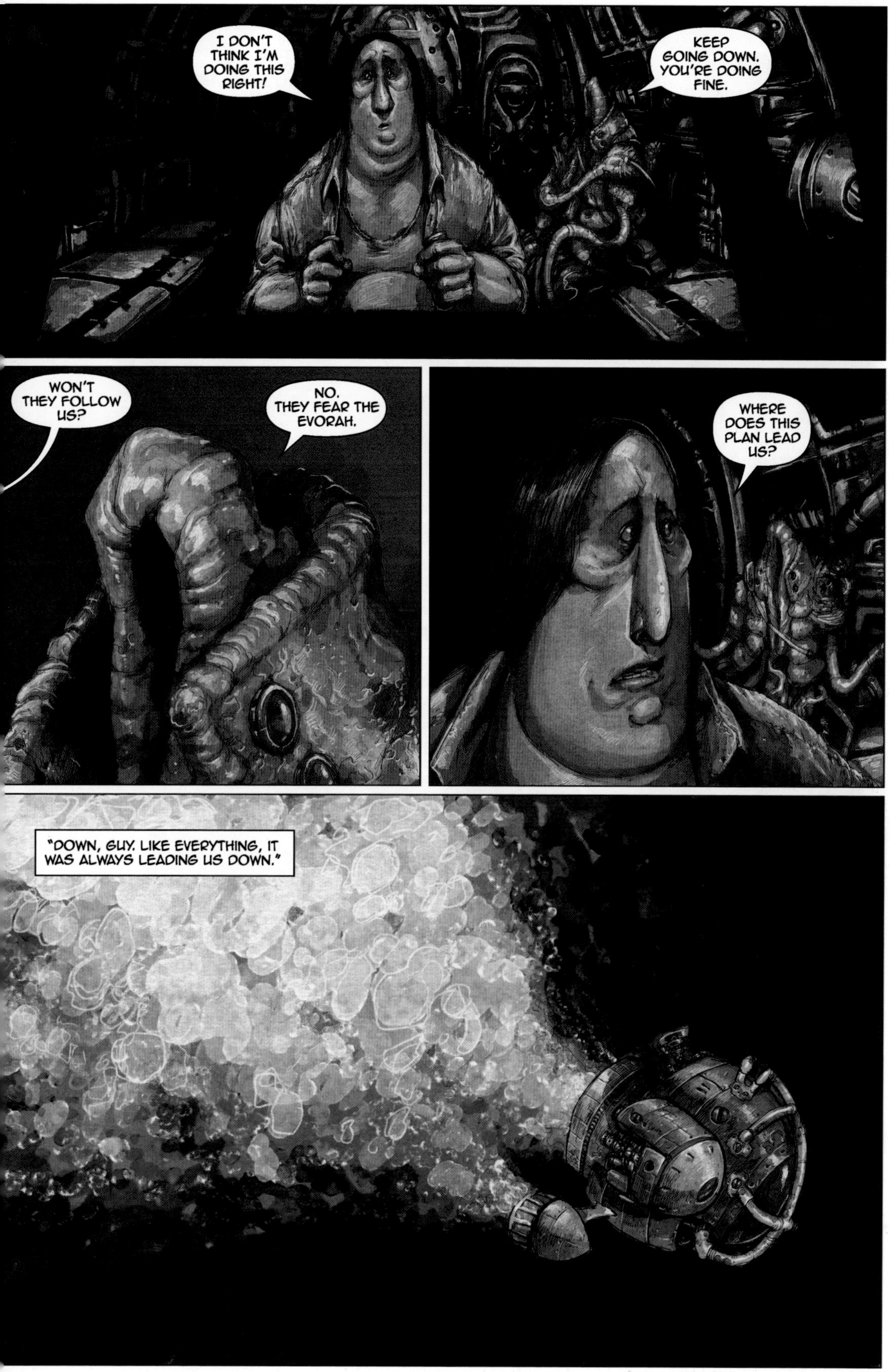
I DON'T THINK I'M DOING THIS RIGHT!
KEEP GOING DOWN. YOU'RE DOING FINE.
WON'T THEY FOLLOW US?
NO. THEY FEAR THE EVORAH.
WHERE DOES THIS PLAN LEAD US?
"DOWN, GUY. LIKE EVERYTHING, IT WAS ALWAYS LEADING US DOWN."

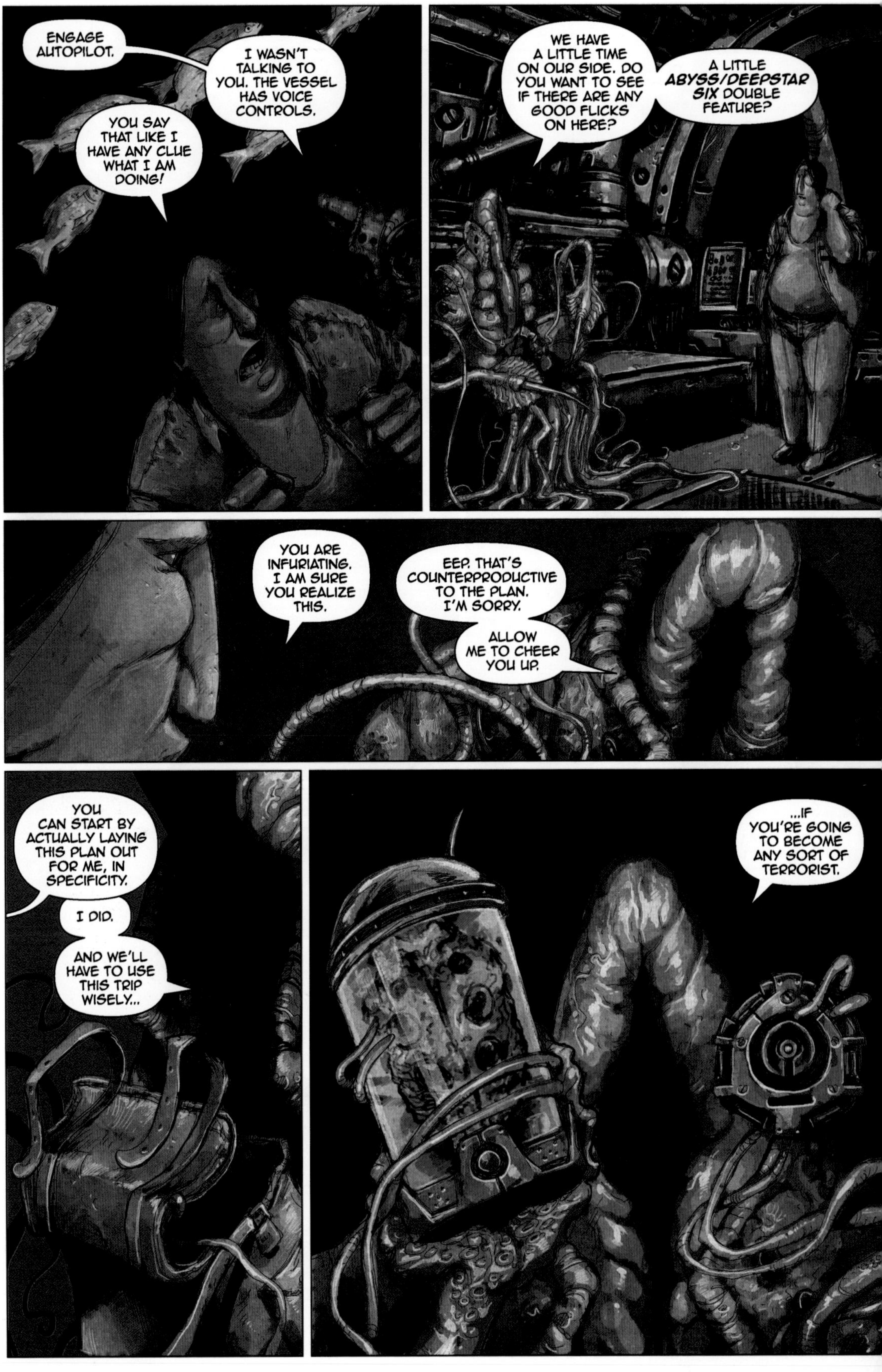
ENGAGE AUTOPILOT.
YOU SAY THAT LIKE I HAVE ANY CLUE WHAT I AM DOING!
I WASN'T TALKING TO YOU. THE VESSEL HAS VOICE CONTROLS.
WE HAVE A LITTLE TIME ON OUR SIDE. DO YOU WANT TO SEE IF THERE ARE ANY GOOD FLICKS ON HERE?
A LITTLE *ABYSS/DEEPSTAR SIX* DOUBLE FEATURE?
YOU ARE INFURIATING. I AM SURE YOU REALIZE THIS.
EEP. THAT'S COUNTERPRODUCTIVE TO THE PLAN. I'M SORRY.
ALLOW ME TO CHEER YOU UP.
YOU CAN START BY ACTUALLY LAYING THIS PLAN OUT FOR ME, IN SPECIFICITY.
I DID.
AND WE'LL HAVE TO USE THIS TRIP WISELY...
...IF YOU'RE GOING TO BECOME ANY SORT OF TERRORIST.

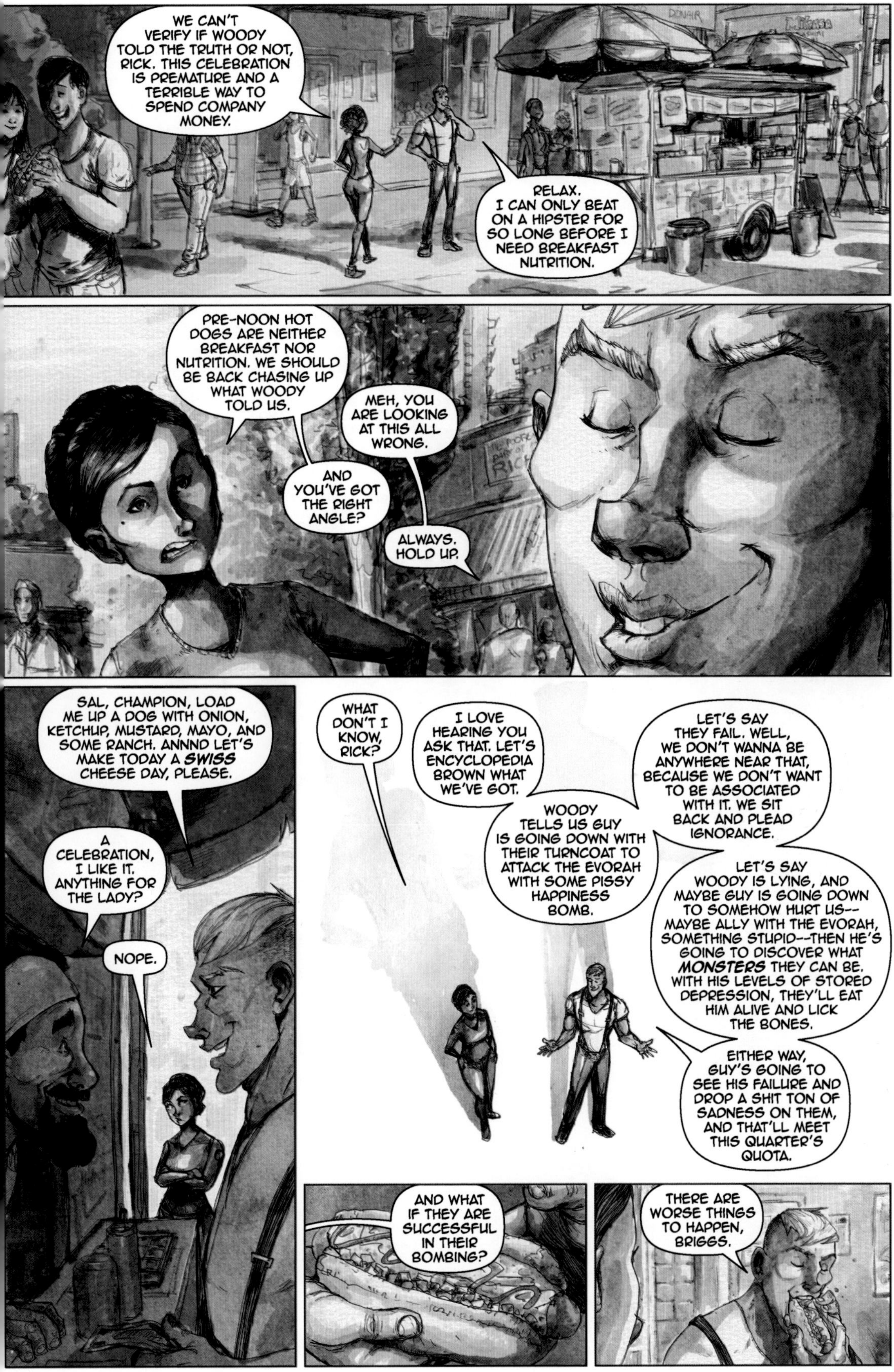
WE CAN'T VERIFY IF WOODY TOLD THE TRUTH OR NOT, RICK. THIS CELEBRATION IS PREMATURE AND A TERRIBLE WAY TO SPEND COMPANY MONEY.
RELAX. I CAN ONLY BEAT ON A HIPSTER FOR SO LONG BEFORE I NEED BREAKFAST NUTRITION.
PRE-NOON HOT DOGS ARE NEITHER BREAKFAST NOR NUTRITION. WE SHOULD BE BACK CHASING UP WHAT WOODY TOLD US.
MEH, YOU ARE LOOKING AT THIS ALL WRONG.
AND YOU'VE GOT THE RIGHT ANGLE?
ALWAYS. HOLD UP.
SAL, CHAMPION, LOAD ME UP A DOG WITH ONION, KETCHUP, MUSTARD, MAYO, AND SOME RANCH. ANNND LET'S MAKE TODAY A *SWISS* CHEESE DAY, PLEASE.
A CELEBRATION, I LIKE IT. ANYTHING FOR THE LADY?
NOPE.
WHAT DON'T I KNOW, RICK?
I LOVE HEARING YOU ASK THAT. LET'S ENCYCLOPEDIA BROWN WHAT WE'VE GOT.
WOODY TELLS US GUY IS GOING DOWN WITH THEIR TURNCOAT TO ATTACK THE EVORAH WITH SOME PISSY HAPPINESS BOMB.
LET'S SAY THEY FAIL. WELL, WE DON'T WANNA BE ANYWHERE NEAR THAT, BECAUSE WE DON'T WANT TO BE ASSOCIATED WITH IT. WE SIT BACK AND PLEAD IGNORANCE.
LET'S SAY WOODY IS LYING, AND MAYBE GUY IS GOING DOWN TO SOMEHOW HURT US--MAYBE ALLY WITH THE EVORAH, SOMETHING STUPID--THEN HE'S GOING TO DISCOVER WHAT *MONSTERS* THEY CAN BE. WITH HIS LEVELS OF STORED DEPRESSION, THEY'LL EAT HIM ALIVE AND LICK THE BONES.
EITHER WAY, GUY'S GOING TO SEE HIS FAILURE AND DROP A SHIT TON OF SADNESS ON THEM, AND THAT'LL MEET THIS QUARTER'S QUOTA.
AND WHAT IF THEY ARE SUCCESSFUL IN THEIR BOMBING?
THERE ARE WORSE THINGS TO HAPPEN, BRIGGS.

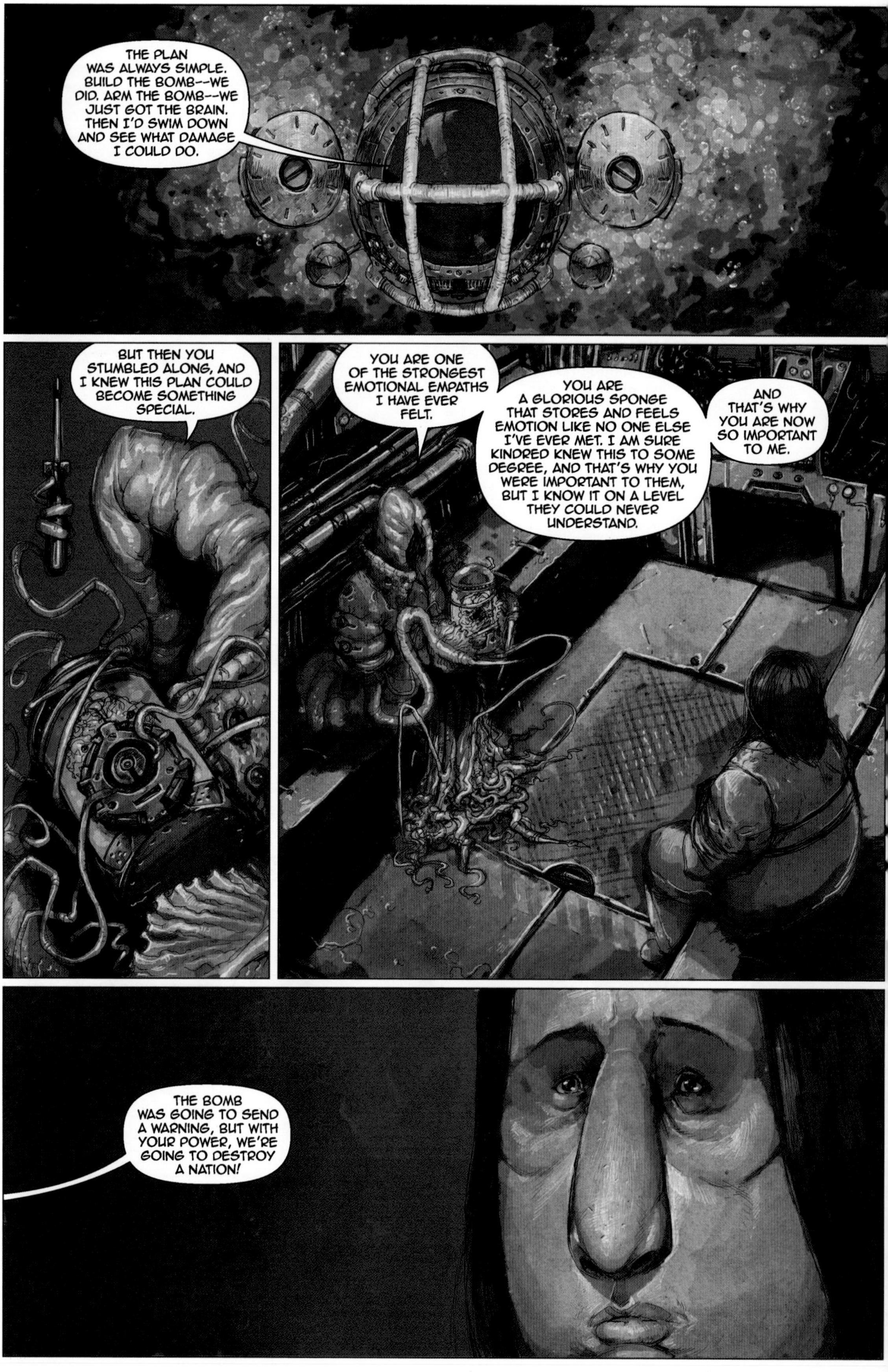
THE PLAN WAS ALWAYS SIMPLE. BUILD THE BOMB--WE DID. ARM THE BOMB--WE JUST GOT THE BRAIN. THEN I'D SWIM DOWN AND SEE WHAT DAMAGE I COULD DO.
BUT THEN YOU STUMBLED ALONG, AND I KNEW THIS PLAN COULD BECOME SOMETHING SPECIAL.
YOU ARE ONE OF THE STRONGEST EMOTIONAL EMPATHS I HAVE EVER FELT.
YOU ARE A GLORIOUS SPONGE THAT STORES AND FEELS EMOTION LIKE NO ONE ELSE I'VE EVER MET. I AM SURE KINDRED KNEW THIS TO SOME DEGREE, AND THAT'S WHY YOU WERE IMPORTANT TO THEM, BUT I KNOW IT ON A LEVEL THEY COULD NEVER UNDERSTAND.
AND THAT'S WHY YOU ARE NOW SO IMPORTANT TO ME.
THE BOMB WAS GOING TO SEND A WARNING, BUT WITH YOUR POWER, WE'RE GOING TO DESTROY A NATION!

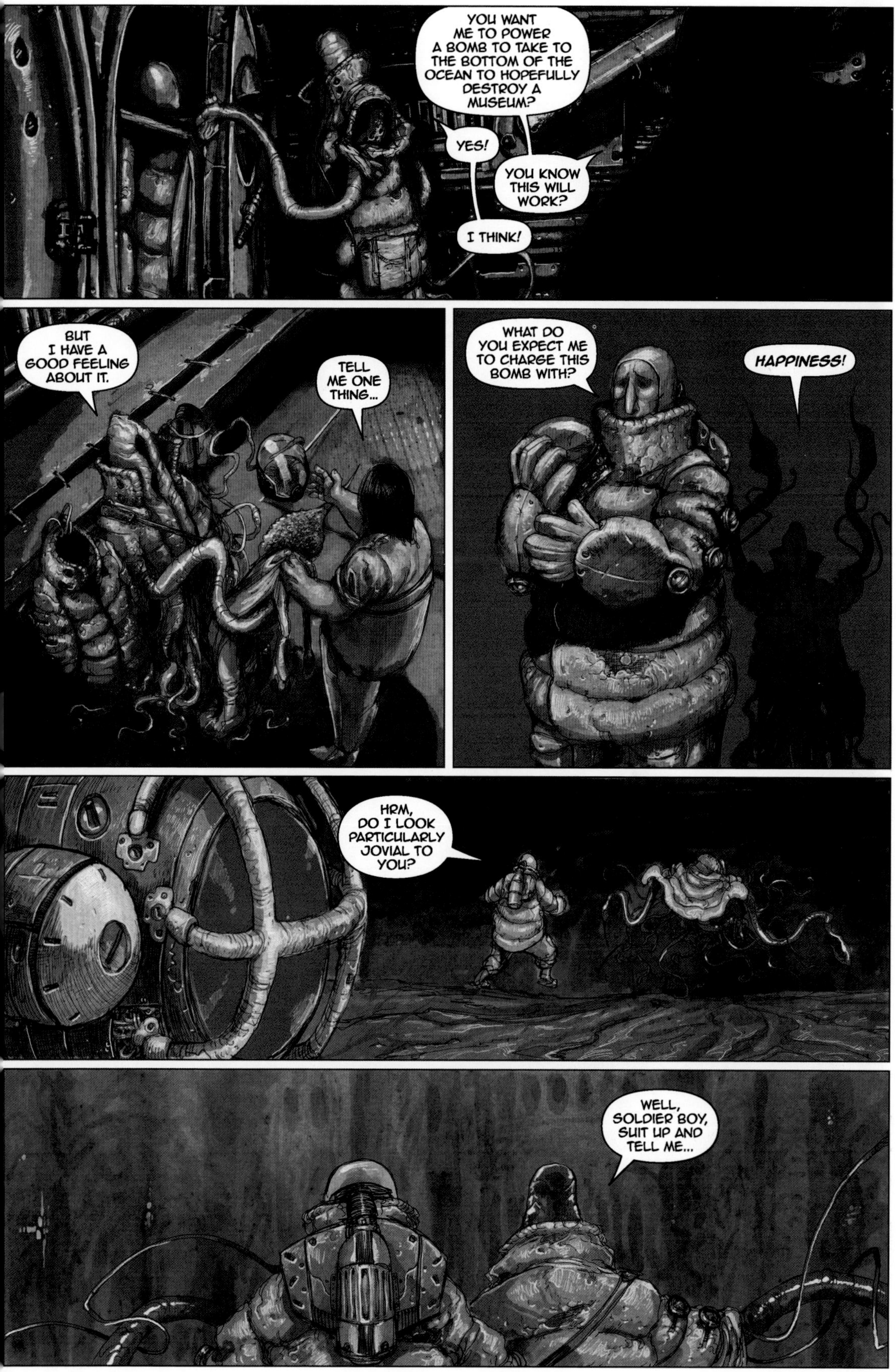
YOU WANT ME TO POWER A BOMB TO TAKE TO THE BOTTOM OF THE OCEAN TO HOPEFULLY DESTROY A MUSEUM?
YES!
YOU KNOW THIS WILL WORK?
I THINK!
BUT I HAVE A GOOD FEELING ABOUT IT.
TELL ME ONE THING...
WHAT DO YOU EXPECT ME TO CHARGE THIS BOMB WITH?
HAPPINESS!
HRM, DO I LOOK PARTICULARLY JOVIAL TO YOU?
WELL, SOLDIER BOY, SUIT UP AND TELL ME...

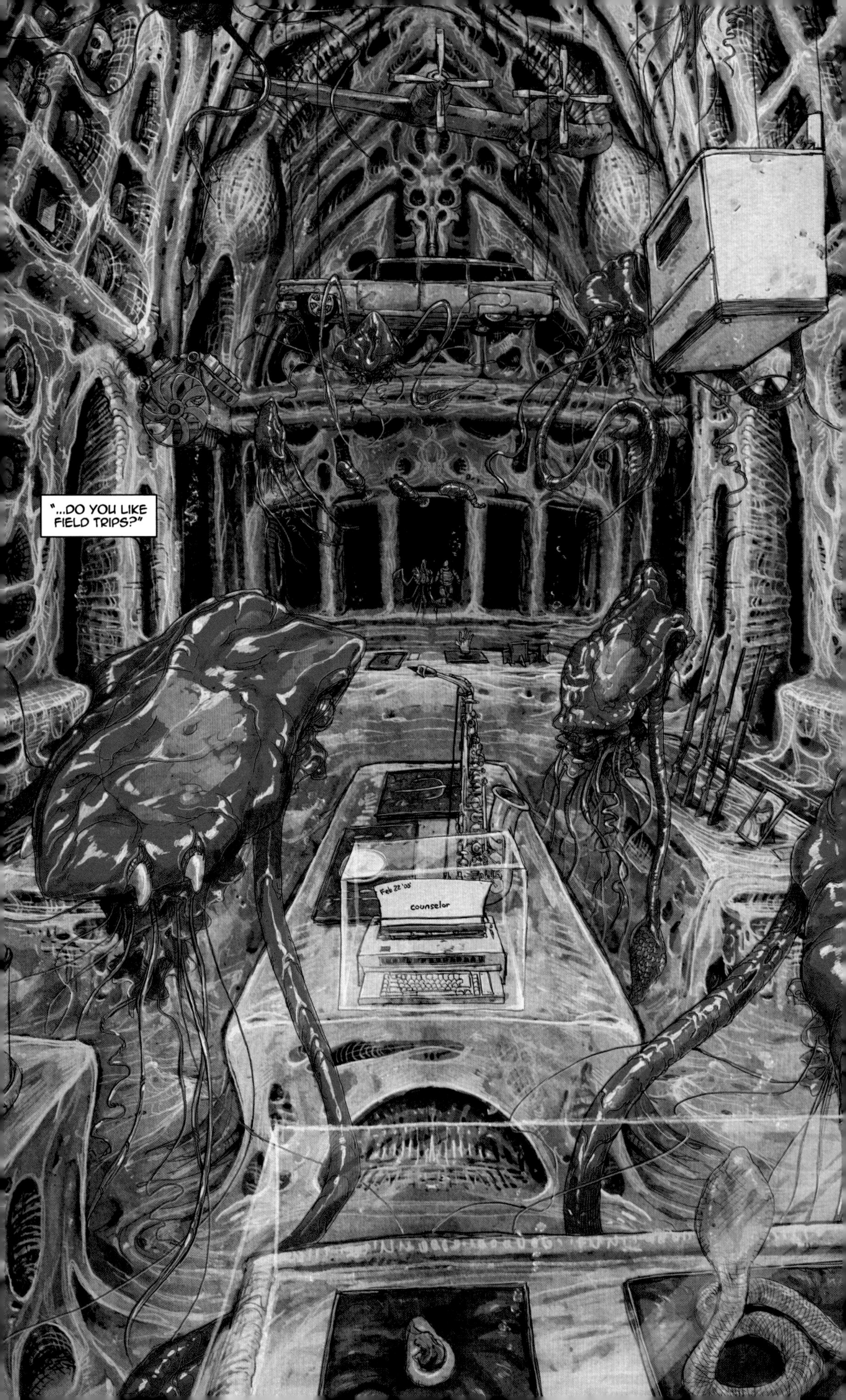
"...DO YOU LIKE FIELD TRIPS?"
Feb 22 '05'
counselor

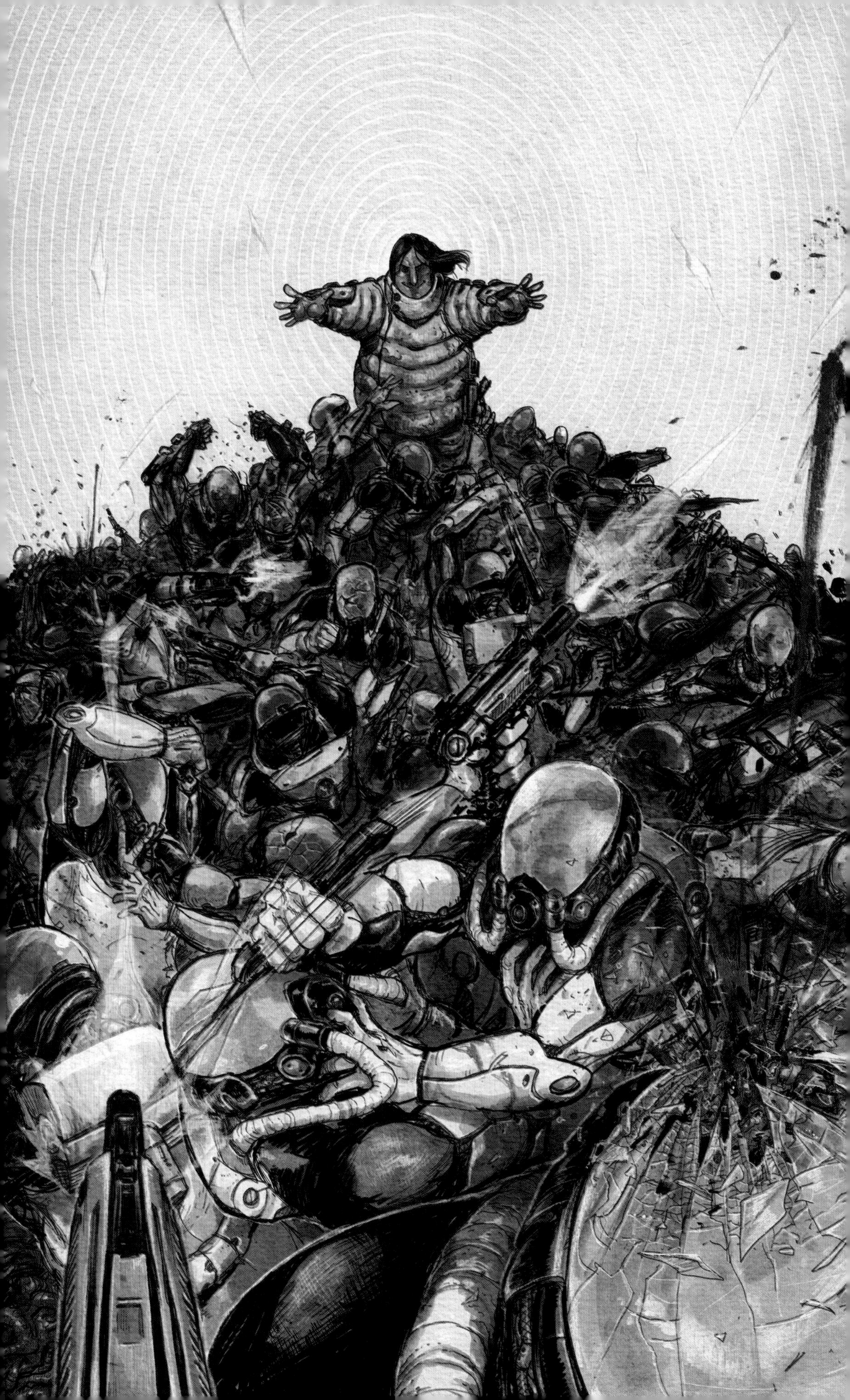

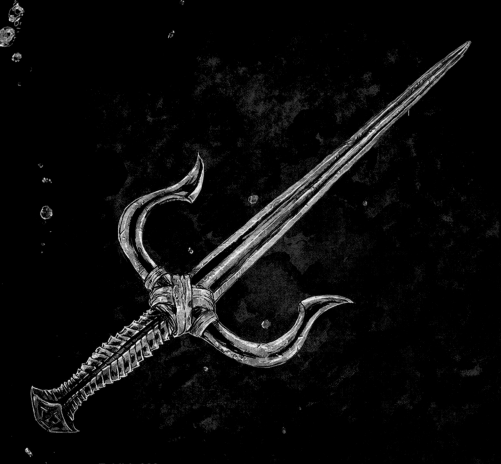

Exhibit 623
Midori's Sai

Midori Yasimoto fought a one-woman war across Japan to be reunited with her childhood love. Upon her arrival, her lover's brother took her in to help her prepare for the blessed reunion. As she bathed alone, thinking of finally holding her lover once more, the brother entered the room and stabbed her with her own sai. He then set fire to the entire property and was never seen again, but not before he delivered the sai to the Evorah monsters.

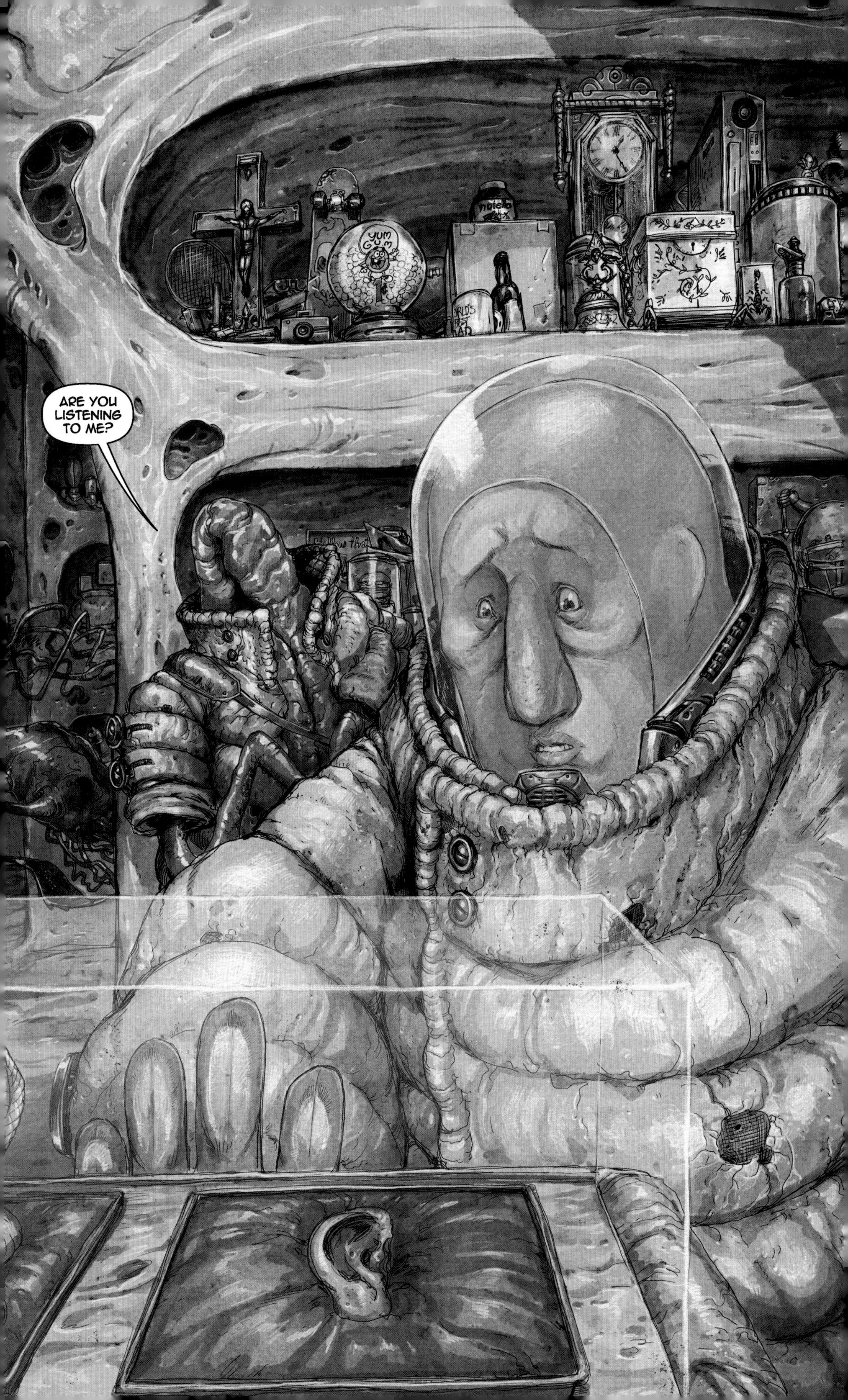
ARE YOU LISTENING TO ME?

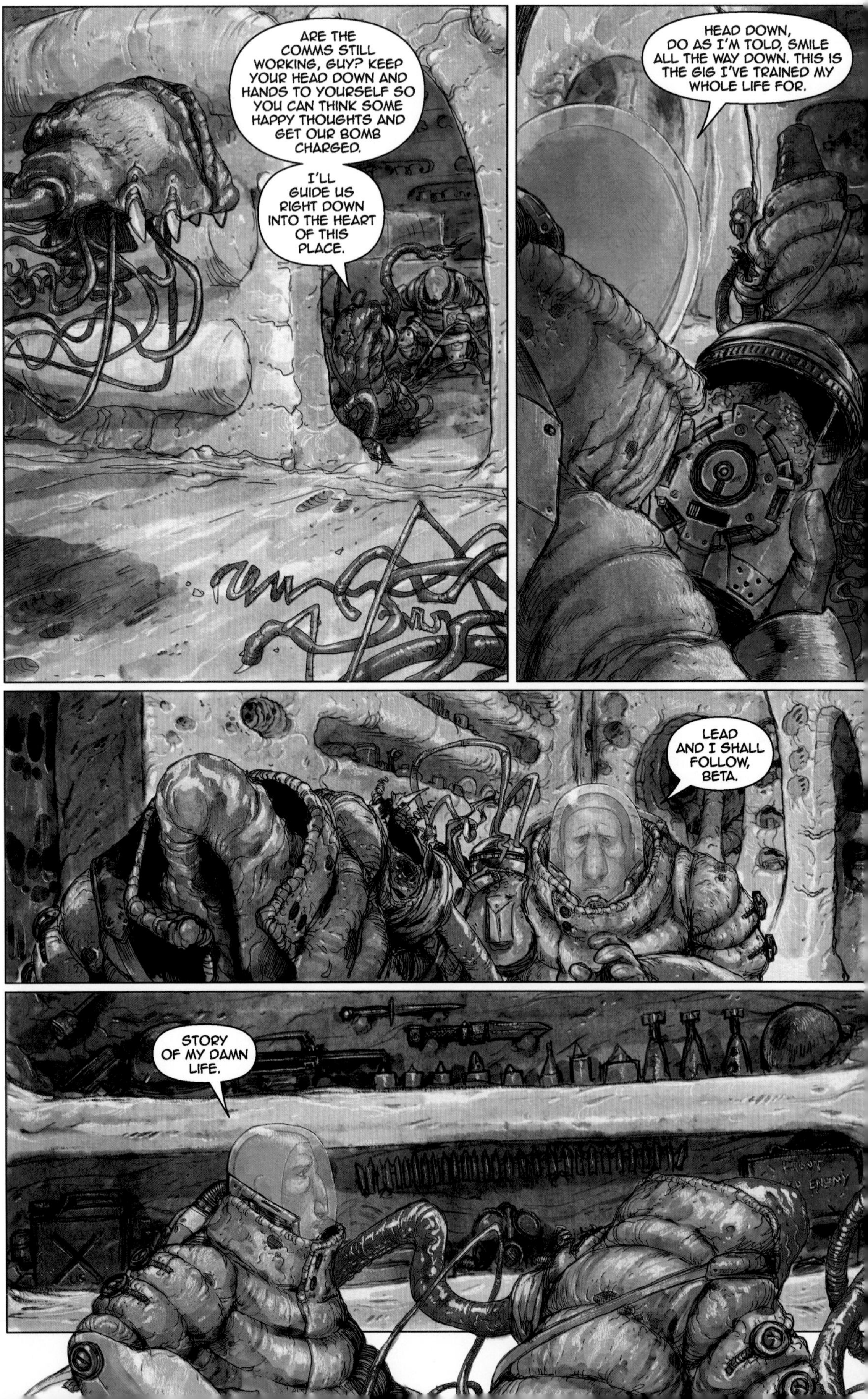
ARE THE COMMS STILL WORKING, GUY? KEEP YOUR HEAD DOWN AND HANDS TO YOURSELF SO YOU CAN THINK SOME HAPPY THOUGHTS AND GET OUR BOMB CHARGED.
I'LL GUIDE US RIGHT DOWN INTO THE HEART OF THIS PLACE.
HEAD DOWN, DO AS I'M TOLD, SMILE ALL THE WAY DOWN. THIS IS THE GIG I'VE TRAINED MY WHOLE LIFE FOR.
LEAD AND I SHALL FOLLOW, BETA.
STORY OF MY DAMN LIFE.

SHHHHHHH

I FEEL EVERYTHING IN THE ROOM, AND IT'S NOT THEIR DEPRESSION THAT GETS TO ME--IT'S THEIR SOMBER INQUISITIVENESS AND RESPECT.

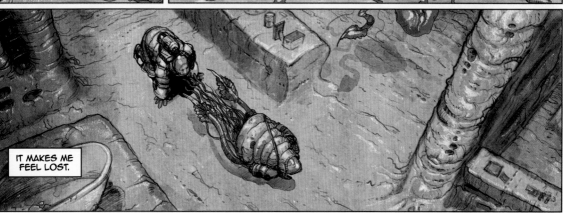

IT MAKES ME FEEL LOST.

AND THEN I FEEL FOUND.

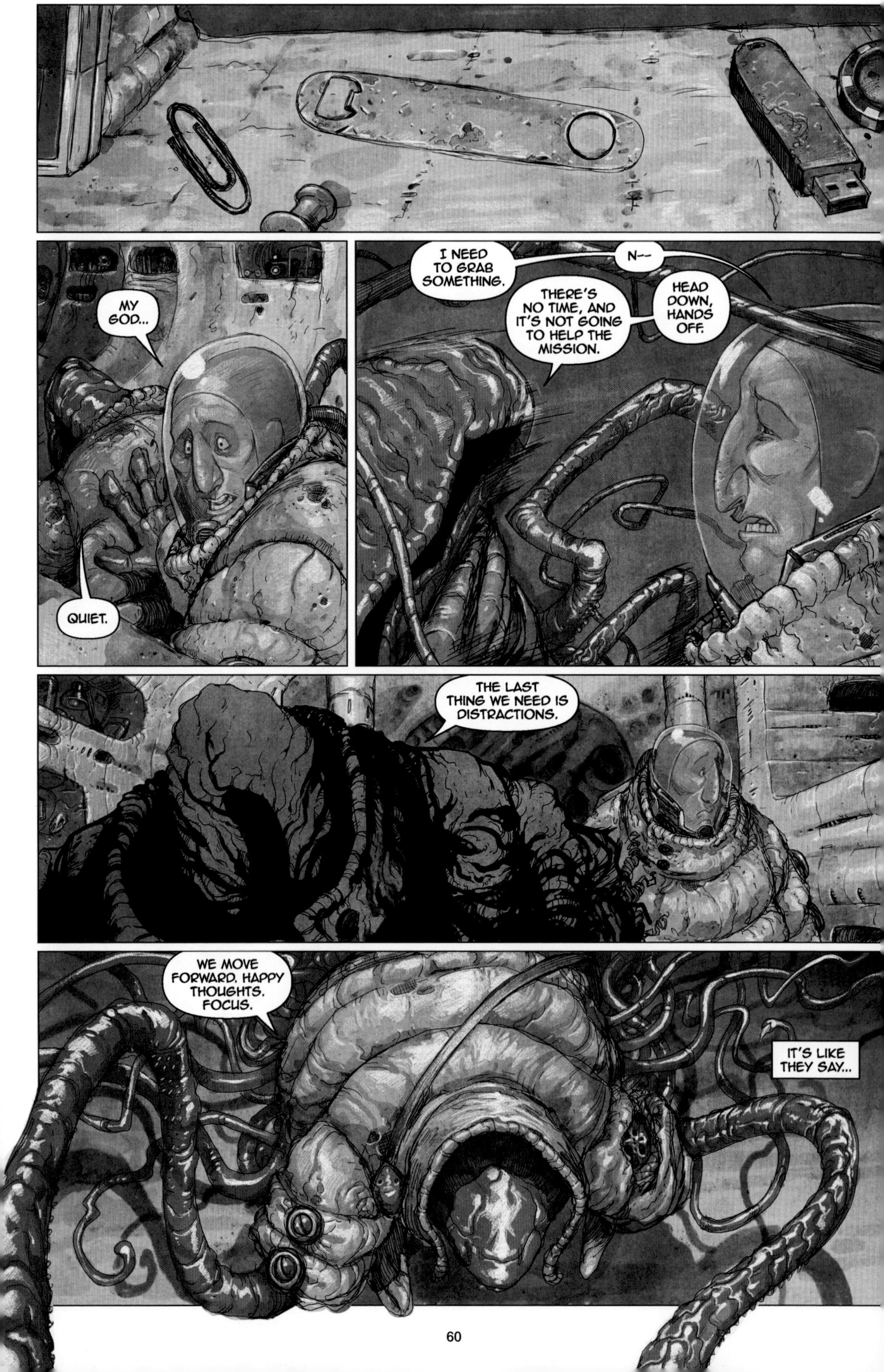
MY GOD...
QUIET.
I NEED TO GRAB SOMETHING.
N--
THERE'S NO TIME, AND IT'S NOT GOING TO HELP THE MISSION.
HEAD DOWN, HANDS OFF.
THE LAST THING WE NEED IS DISTRACTIONS.
WE MOVE FORWARD. HAPPY THOUGHTS. FOCUS.
IT'S LIKE THEY SAY...

...IT'S BETTER TO BEG FORGIVENESS THAN IT IS TO ASK PERMISSION.

SHIT!

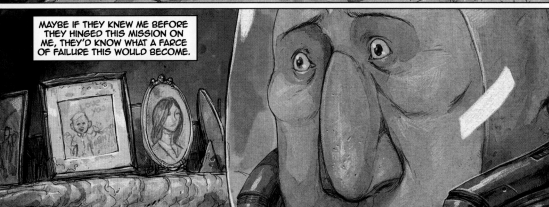

MAYBE IF THEY KNEW ME BEFORE THEY HINGED THIS MISSION ON ME, THEY'D KNOW WHAT A FARCE OF FAILURE THIS WOULD BECOME.

I'M NOT KNOWN FOR MAKING GREAT LIFE DECISIONS.

I CERTAINLY WOULDN'T CHOOSE TO BE MY PARTNER.

THEY MAKE NOISES AT EACH OTHER. IT'S LIKE GRITTY SONAR BUT IT'S WORDS. IT'S NOT CLEAN AT ALL.

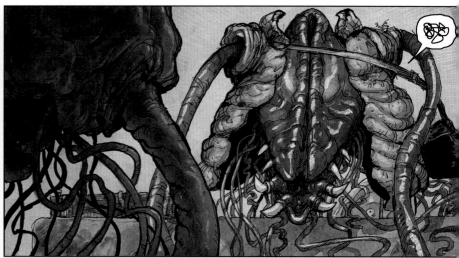

I CAN ONLY HOPE THEY AREN'T TALKING ABOUT ME.

SORRY.

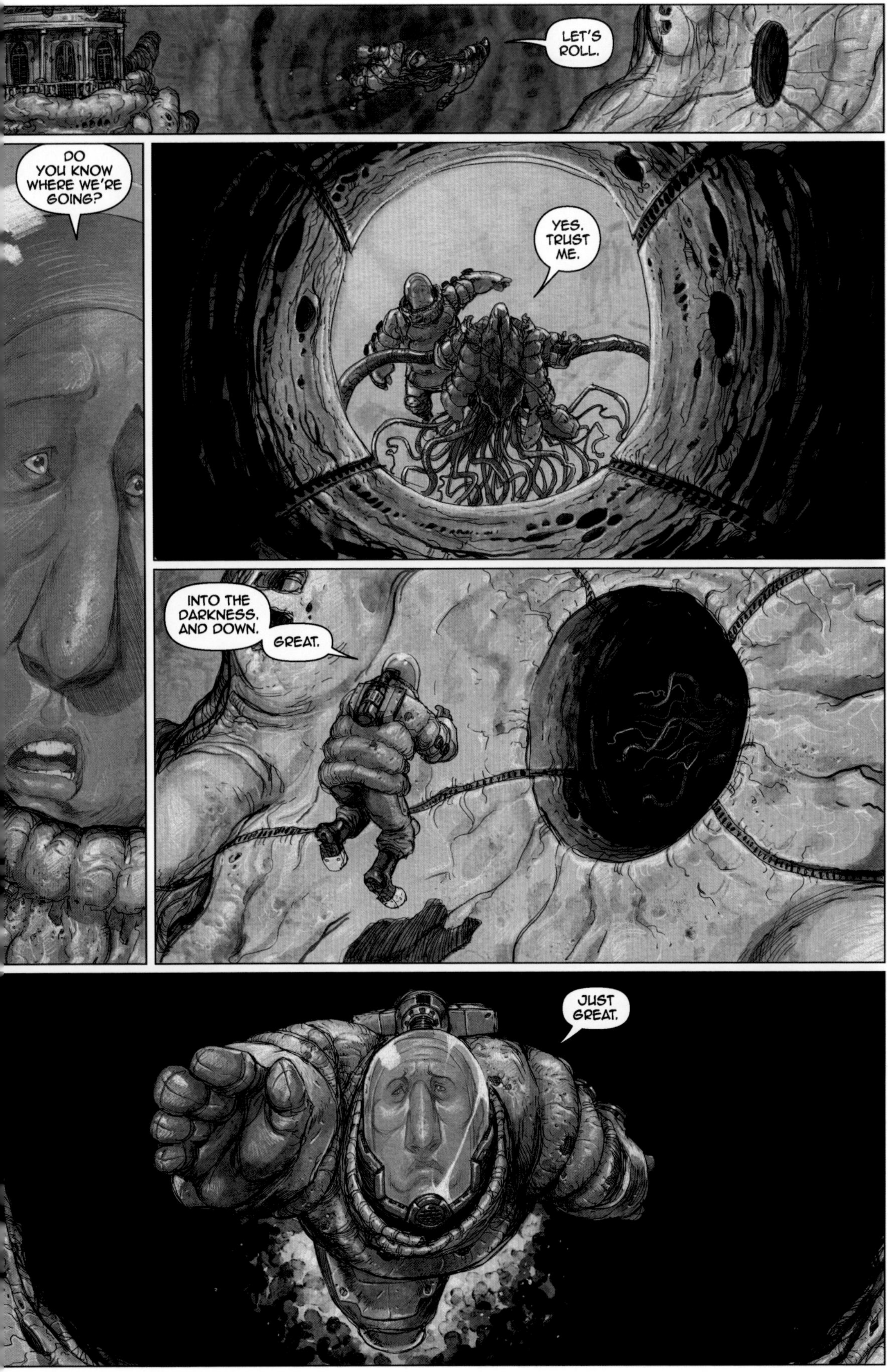
LET'S ROLL.
DO YOU KNOW WHERE WE'RE GOING?
YES. TRUST ME.
INTO THE DARKNESS. AND DOWN.
GREAT.
JUST GREAT.

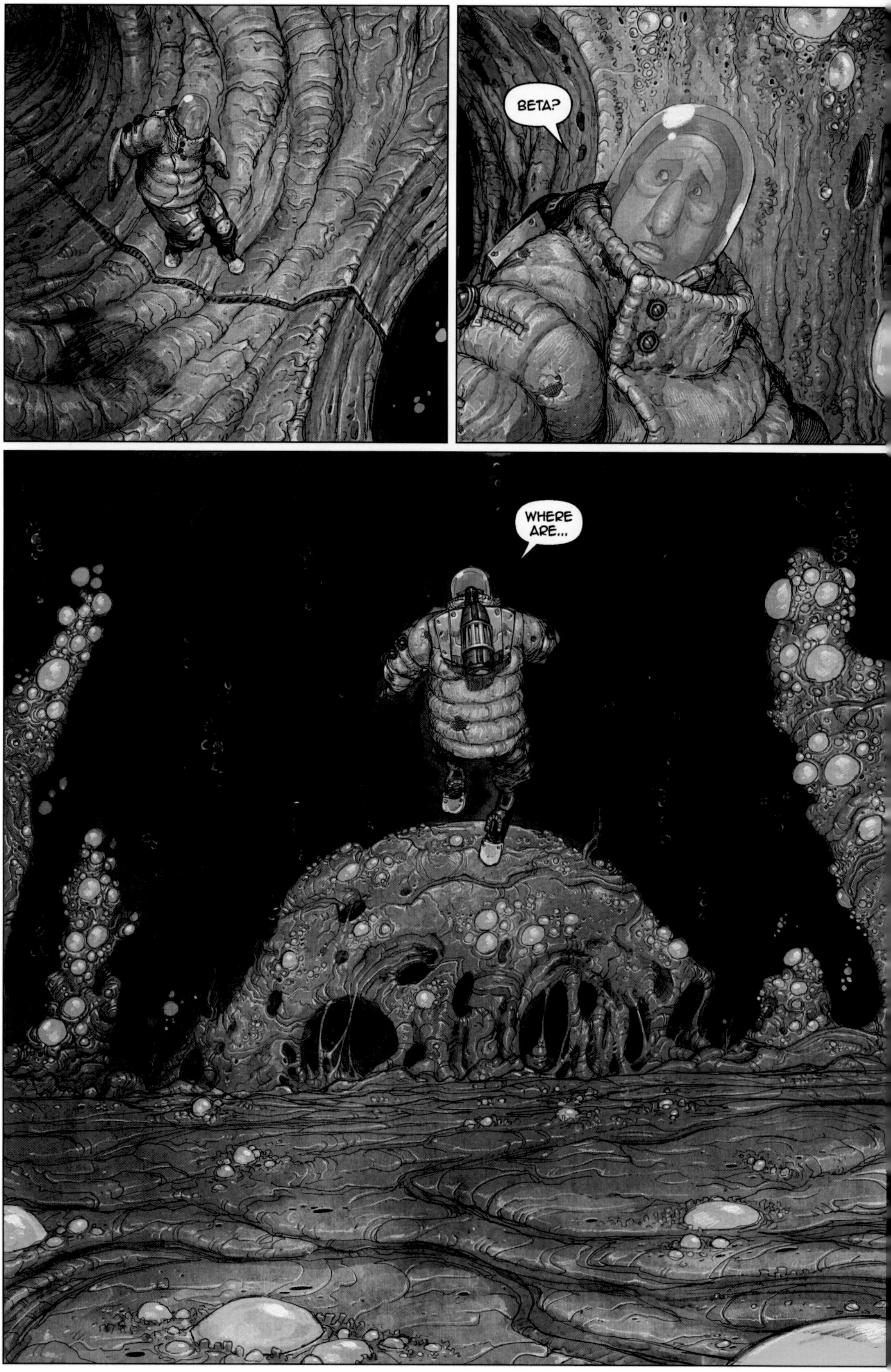
BETA?
WHERE ARE...

...YOU.
WHAT'S IN THERE?
I HAVE NO IDEA.
I THOUGHT YOU KNEW YOUR WAY AROUND HERE.
I DO! THIS SEEMS NEW...
BETA!

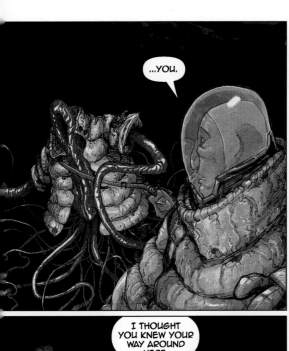

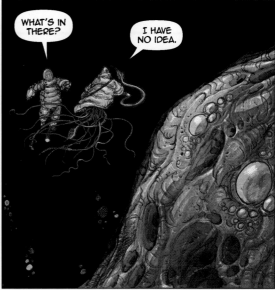

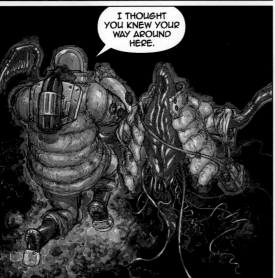

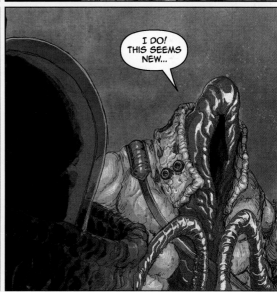

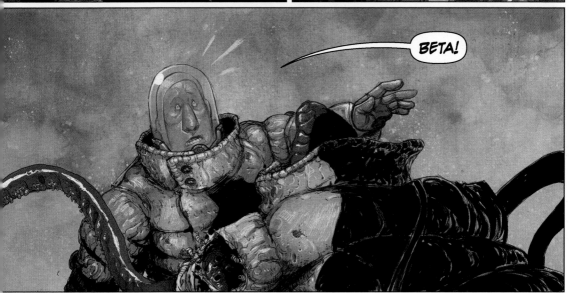

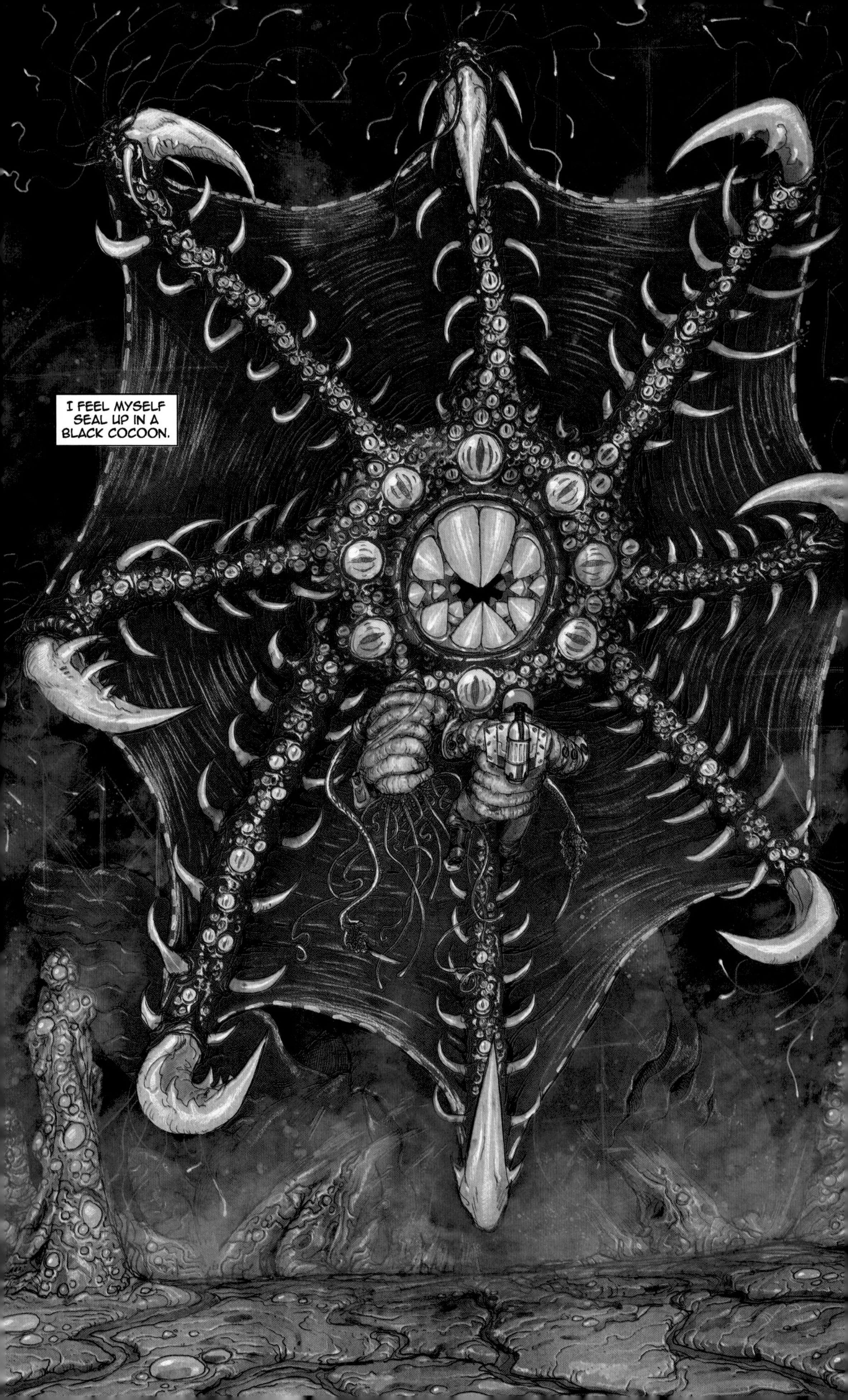
I FEEL MYSELF SEAL UP IN A BLACK COCOON.

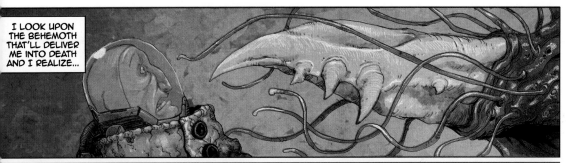

I LOOK UPON THE BEHEMOTH THAT'LL DELIVER ME INTO DEATH AND I REALIZE...

...IT WOULD RATHER KEEP ME AROUND FOR MY MELANCHOLY.

HRRK!

THE TENTACLES TINGLE AND I FEEL IT DRAINING ME OF EMOTION. I DO THE WORST THING A SAD MAN CAN DO...

...I REFLECT.

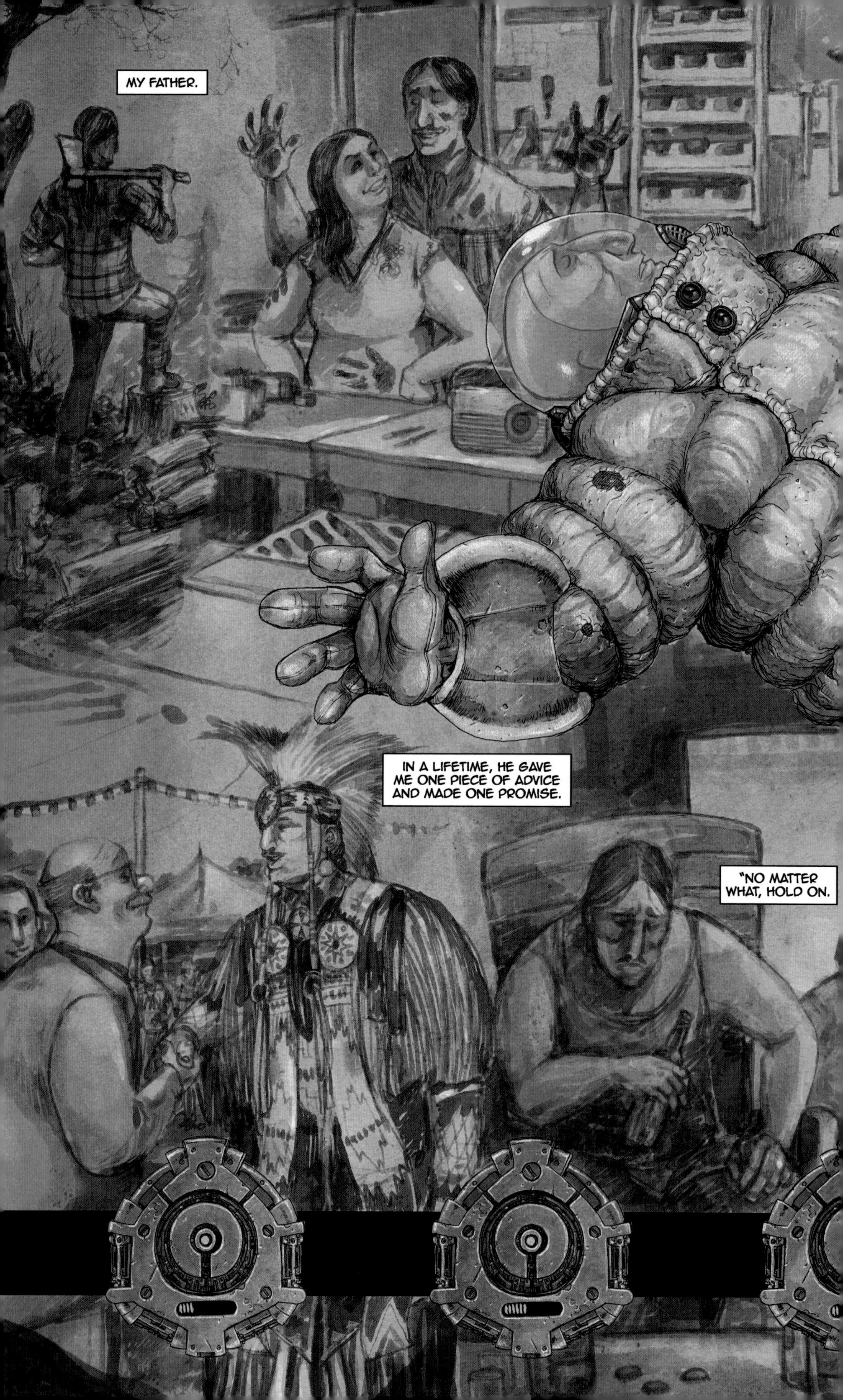
MY FATHER.
IN A LIFETIME, HE GAVE ME ONE PIECE OF ADVICE AND MADE ONE PROMISE.
"NO MATTER WHAT, HOLD ON.

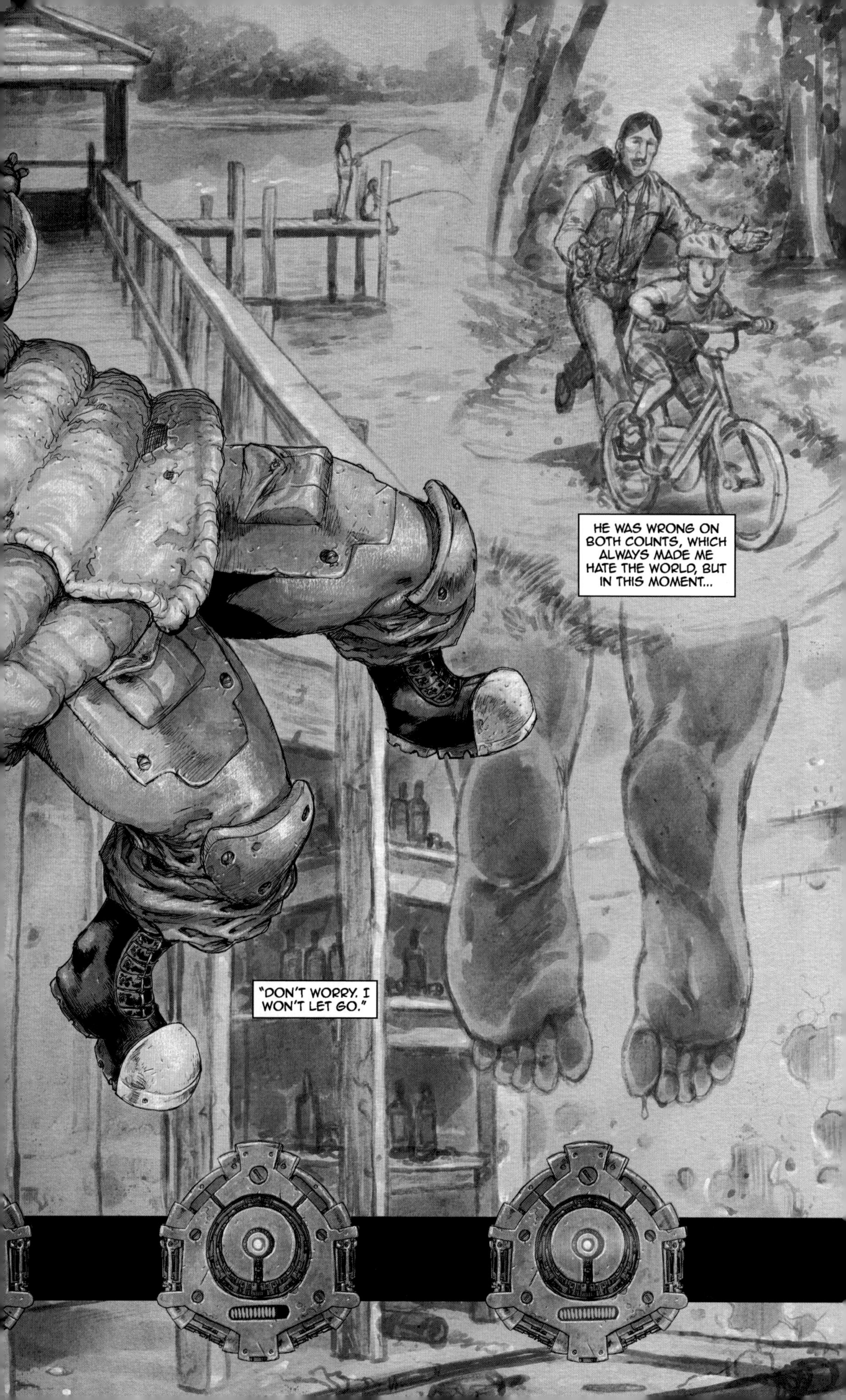
HE WAS WRONG ON BOTH COUNTS, WHICH ALWAYS MADE ME HATE THE WORLD, BUT IN THIS MOMENT...
"DON'T WORRY. I WON'T LET GO."

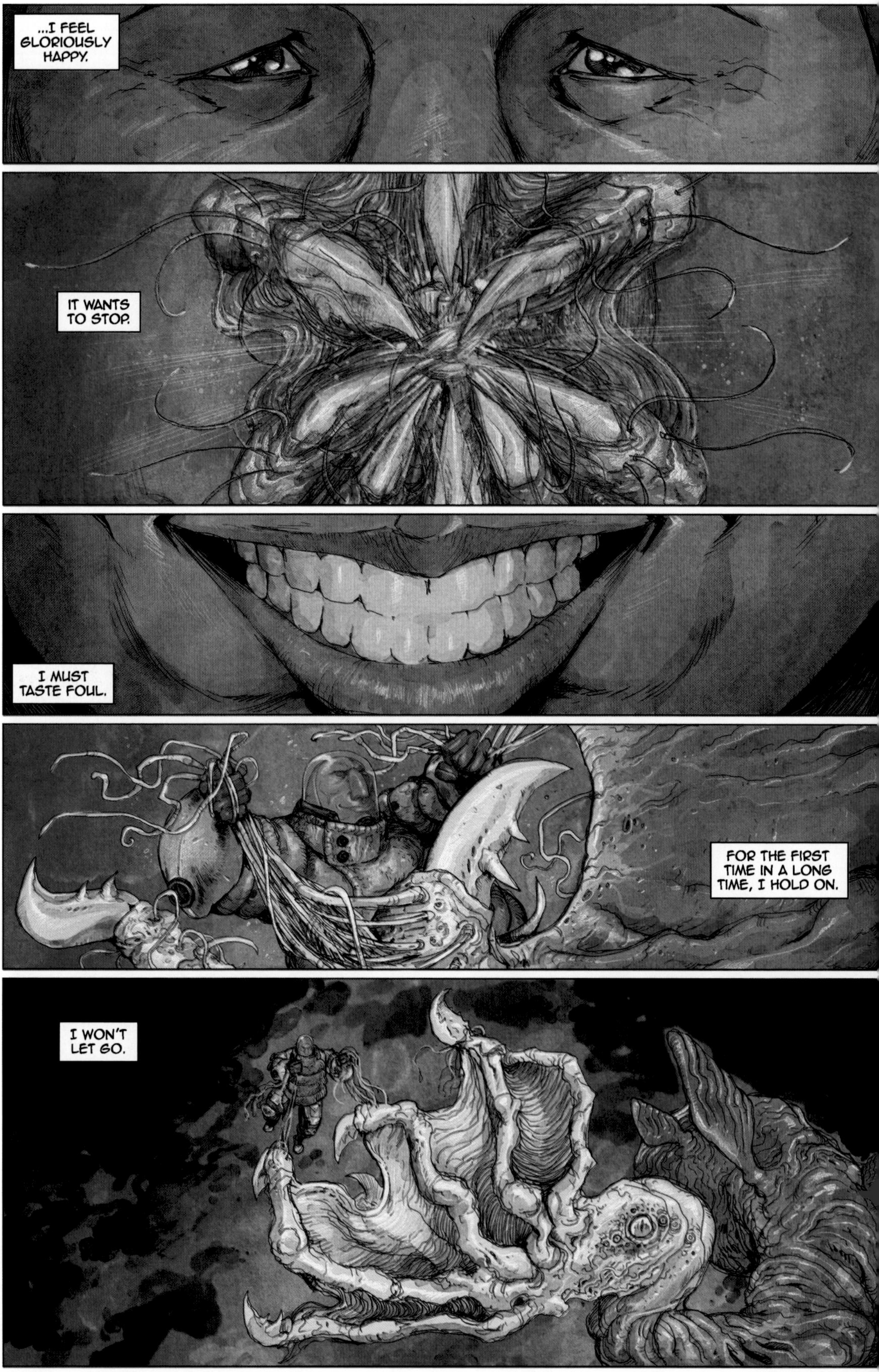
...I FEEL GLORIOUSLY HAPPY.
IT WANTS TO STOP.
I MUST TASTE FOUL.
FOR THE FIRST TIME IN A LONG TIME, I HOLD ON.
I WON'T LET GO.

THE BOMB IS CHARGED, YOU'VE SAVED THE DAY, MY GODDAMN GUNSHOT WOUND IS HEALED, AND I THINK I JUST FELL IN LOVE WITH YOU.

WHAT THE *HELL* WERE YOU THINKING ABOUT FOR THE HAPPINESS TO RUN OUT OF YOU LIKE THAT?

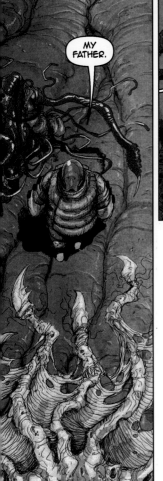

MY FATHER.

LET'S DETONATE THE BOMB AND THEN I DO BELIEVE I OWE YOUR OLD MAN A BIG WET KISS ONCE WE GET TOPSIDE. *YOU* DO THE HONORS.

...

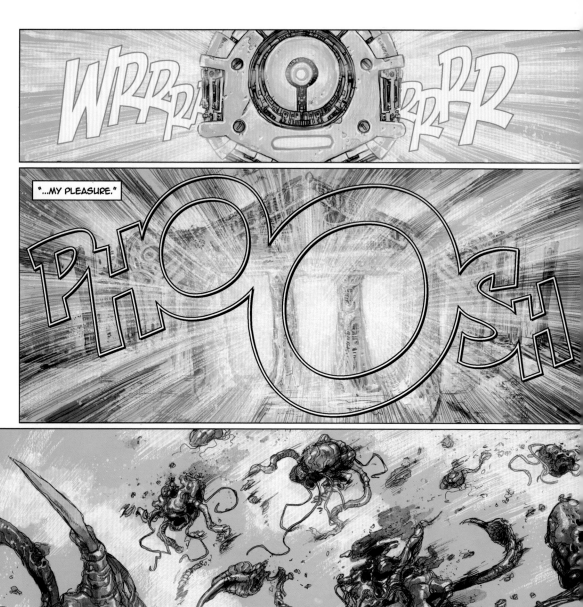

"...MY PLEASURE."

WRRRRRRR

PHOOOSH

THIS IS HOW ANGELS MUST FEEL.

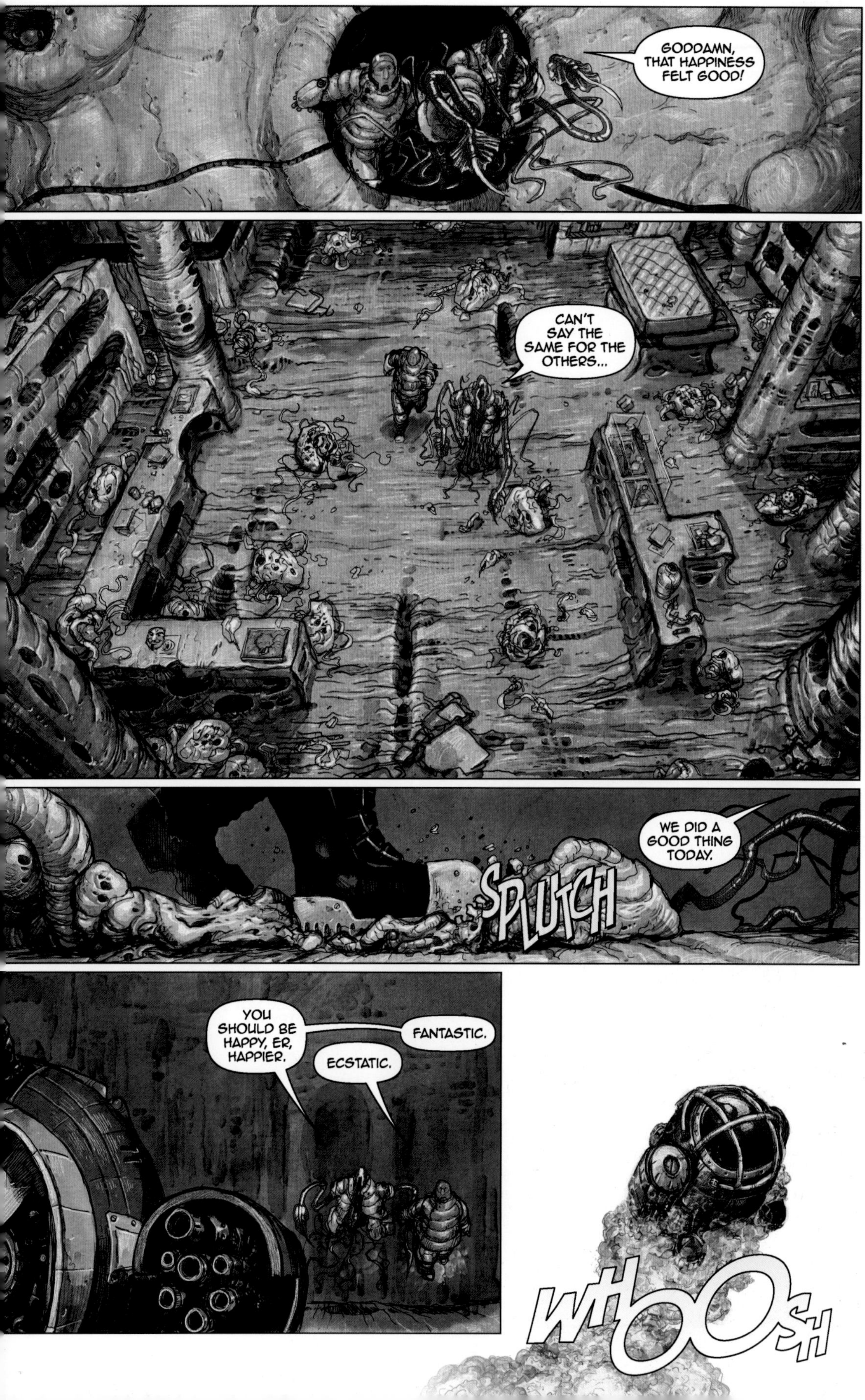
GODDAMN, THAT HAPPINESS FELT GOOD!
CAN'T SAY THE SAME FOR THE OTHERS...
WE DID A GOOD THING TODAY.
SPLUTCH
YOU SHOULD BE HAPPY, ER, HAPPIER.
FANTASTIC.
ECSTATIC.
WHOOSH

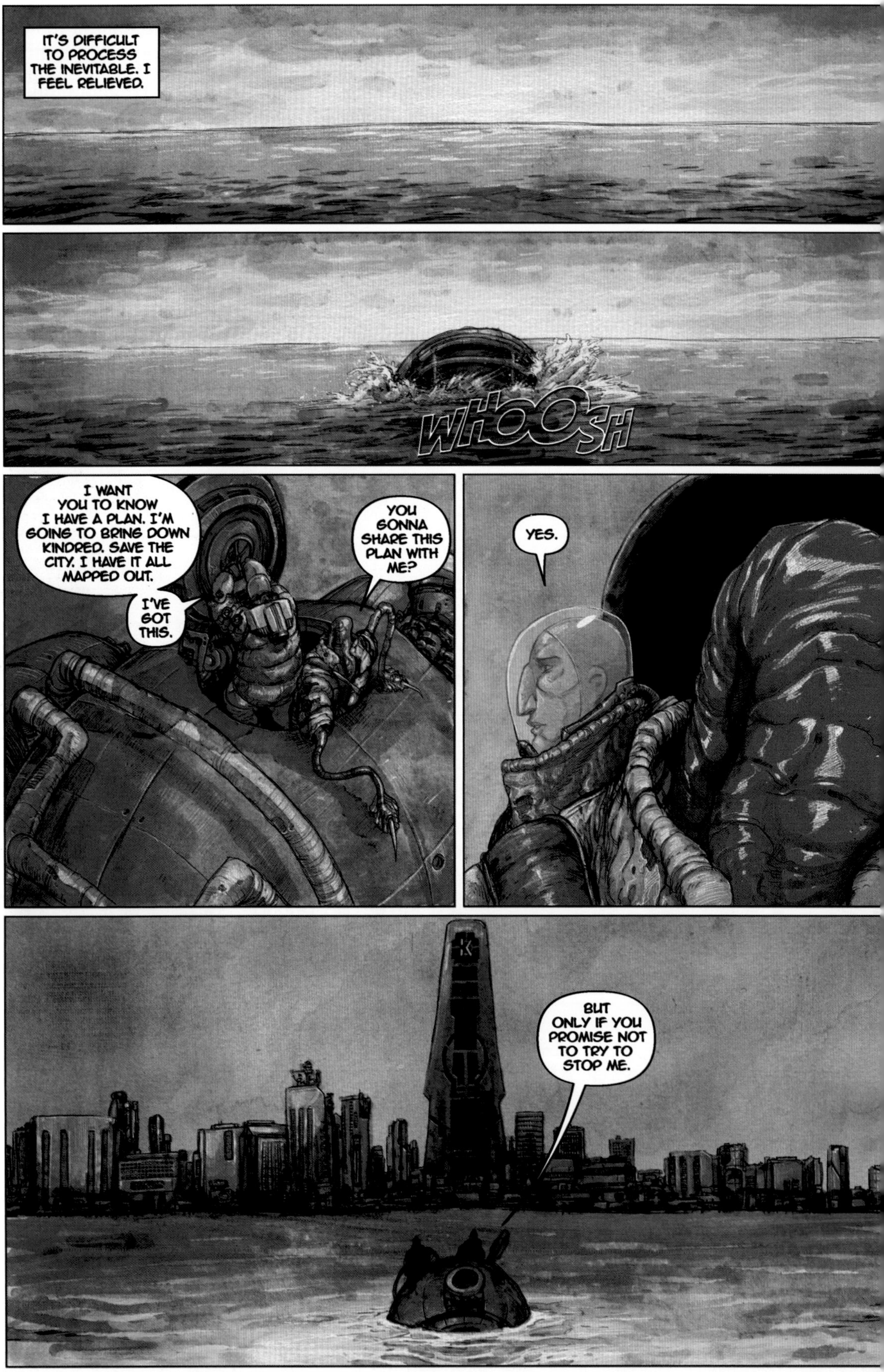
IT'S DIFFICULT TO PROCESS THE INEVITABLE. I FEEL RELIEVED.
WHOOOSH
I WANT YOU TO KNOW I HAVE A PLAN. I'M GOING TO BRING DOWN KINDRED. SAVE THE CITY. I HAVE IT ALL MAPPED OUT.
I'VE GOT THIS.
YOU GONNA SHARE THIS PLAN WITH ME?
YES.
BUT ONLY IF YOU PROMISE NOT TO TRY TO STOP ME.

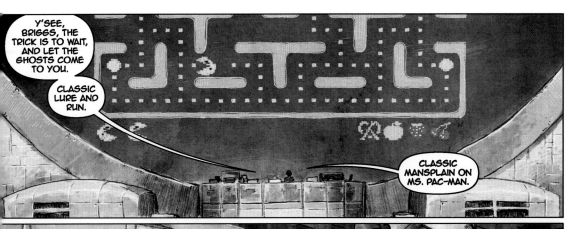

Y'SEE, BRIGGS, THE TRICK IS TO WAIT, AND LET THE GHOSTS COME TO YOU.

CLASSIC LURE AND RUN.

CLASSIC MANSPLAIN ON MS. PAC-MAN.

YOU THINK YOU *ARE* MS. PAC-MAN, DON'T YOU?

PFFT, I'M ONE OF THE GHOSTS. HELL, I'M THE GAME. WE BOTH ARE.

MS. PAC-MAN IS DEPRESSION. EATING THOSE BALLS, THE SAME THINGS, NONSTOP, AND IF YOU DO IT WELL ENOUGH YOU GET TO EAT THE SAME BALLS IN A NEW STUPID ROOM.

THAT SHIT IS FOR THE BIRDS, MAN. WE ARE THE GHOSTS, CORRALLING, WAITING, ALWAYS THERE. AND IN THE END, WE ARE LEGION, AND WE WIN, BECAUSE THE WORLD IS A NEVER-ENDING PARADE OF THE SAME ROOM WITH THE SAME BALLS STUFFED IN YOUR MOUTH.

YOU HEAR THE WORDS AS YOU SAY THEM, RIGHT?

I REGRET NOTHING.

OH.

BZZ BZZ

GUY'S BEEN SIGHTED!

HE'S DOWNSTAIRS, *NOW!*

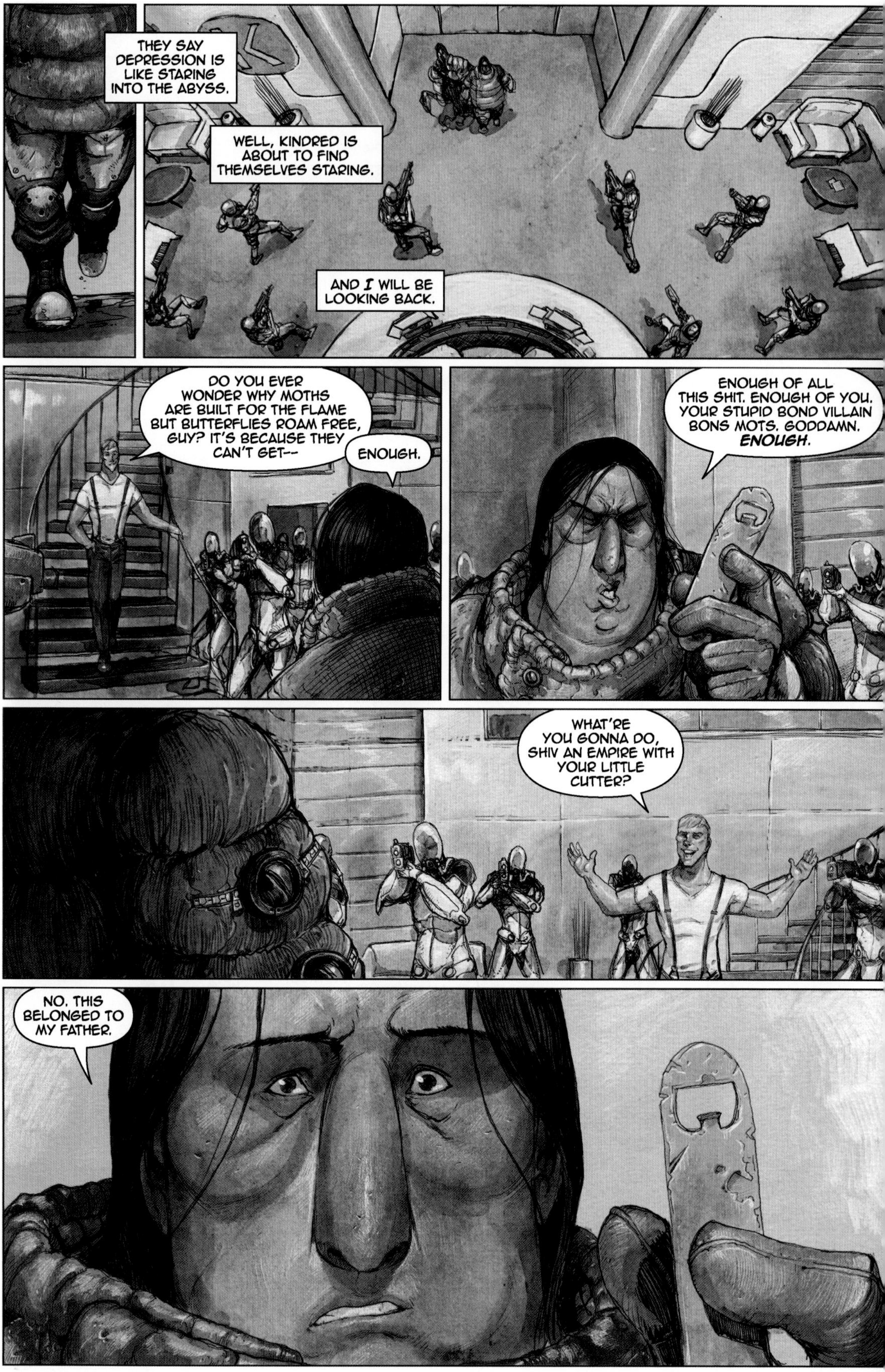

THEY SAY DEPRESSION IS LIKE STARING INTO THE ABYSS.
WELL, KINDRED IS ABOUT TO FIND THEMSELVES STARING.
AND *I* WILL BE LOOKING BACK.
DO YOU EVER WONDER WHY MOTHS ARE BUILT FOR THE FLAME BUT BUTTERFLIES ROAM FREE, GUY? IT'S BECAUSE THEY CAN'T GET--
ENOUGH.
ENOUGH OF ALL THIS SHIT. ENOUGH OF YOU. YOUR STUPID BOND VILLAIN BONS MOTS. GODDAMN. ***ENOUGH***.
WHAT'RE YOU GONNA DO, SHIV AN EMPIRE WITH YOUR LITTLE CUTTER?
NO. THIS BELONGED TO MY FATHER.

"I CUT HIM DOWN WITH IT."

AND EVER SINCE I'VE BEEN HOLDING IT, I'VE HAD THIS GHASTLY MEMORY, AND IT'S BEEN MAKING ME TERRIBLY HAPPY.

YOU SEE...

HOLDING THIS REMINDS ME HOW MUCH I LOVED HIM AND MISS HIM.

ALL I CAN THINK ABOUT IS GETTING TO SEE HIM SOON.

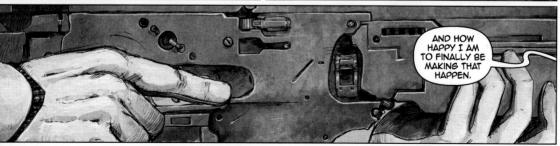

AND HOW HAPPY I AM TO FINALLY BE MAKING THAT HAPPEN.

THIS IS IT. I AM FINISHED...

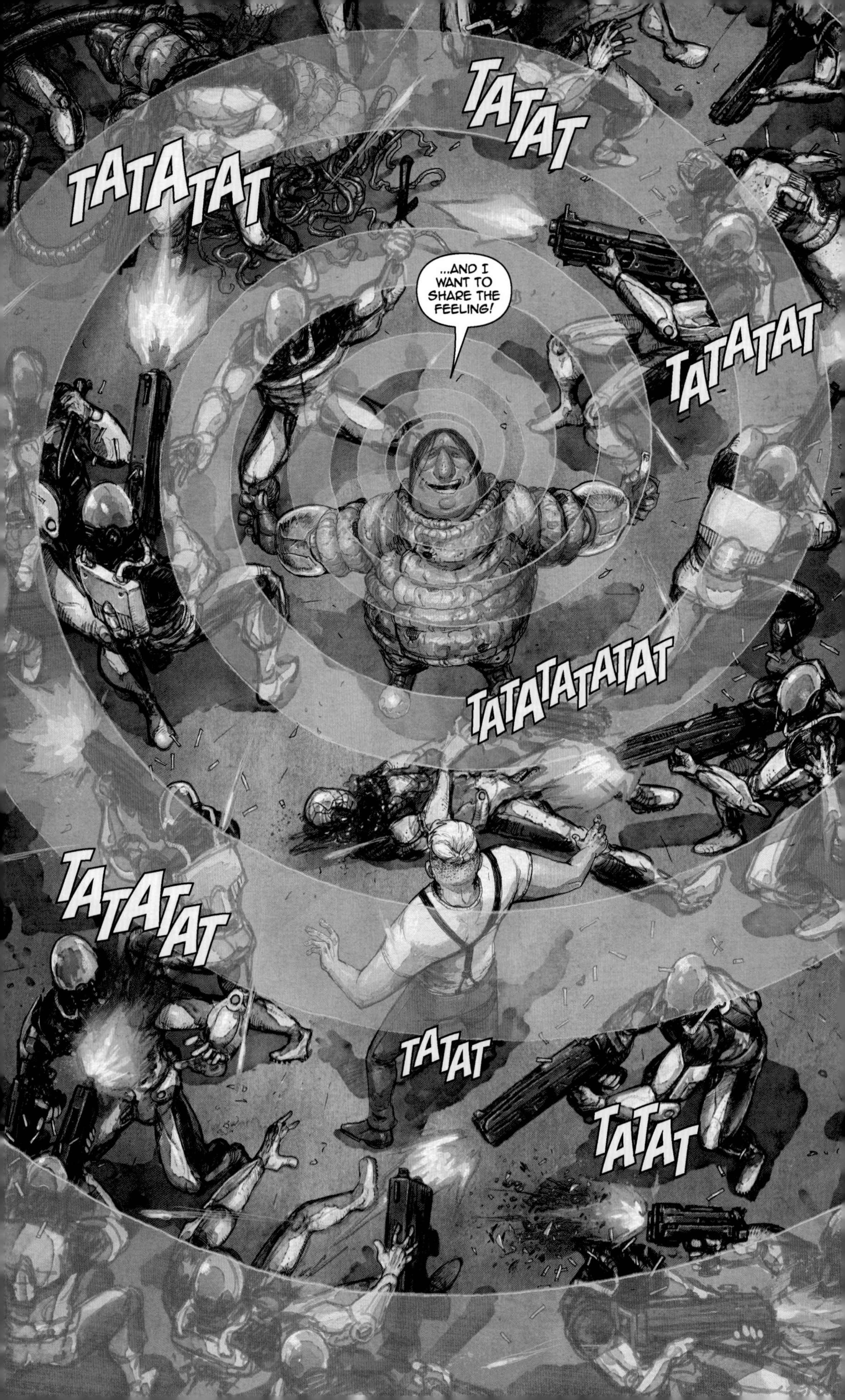
TATATAT
TATAT
...AND I WANT TO SHARE THE FEELING!
TATATAT
TATATATATAT
TATATAT
TATAT
TATAT

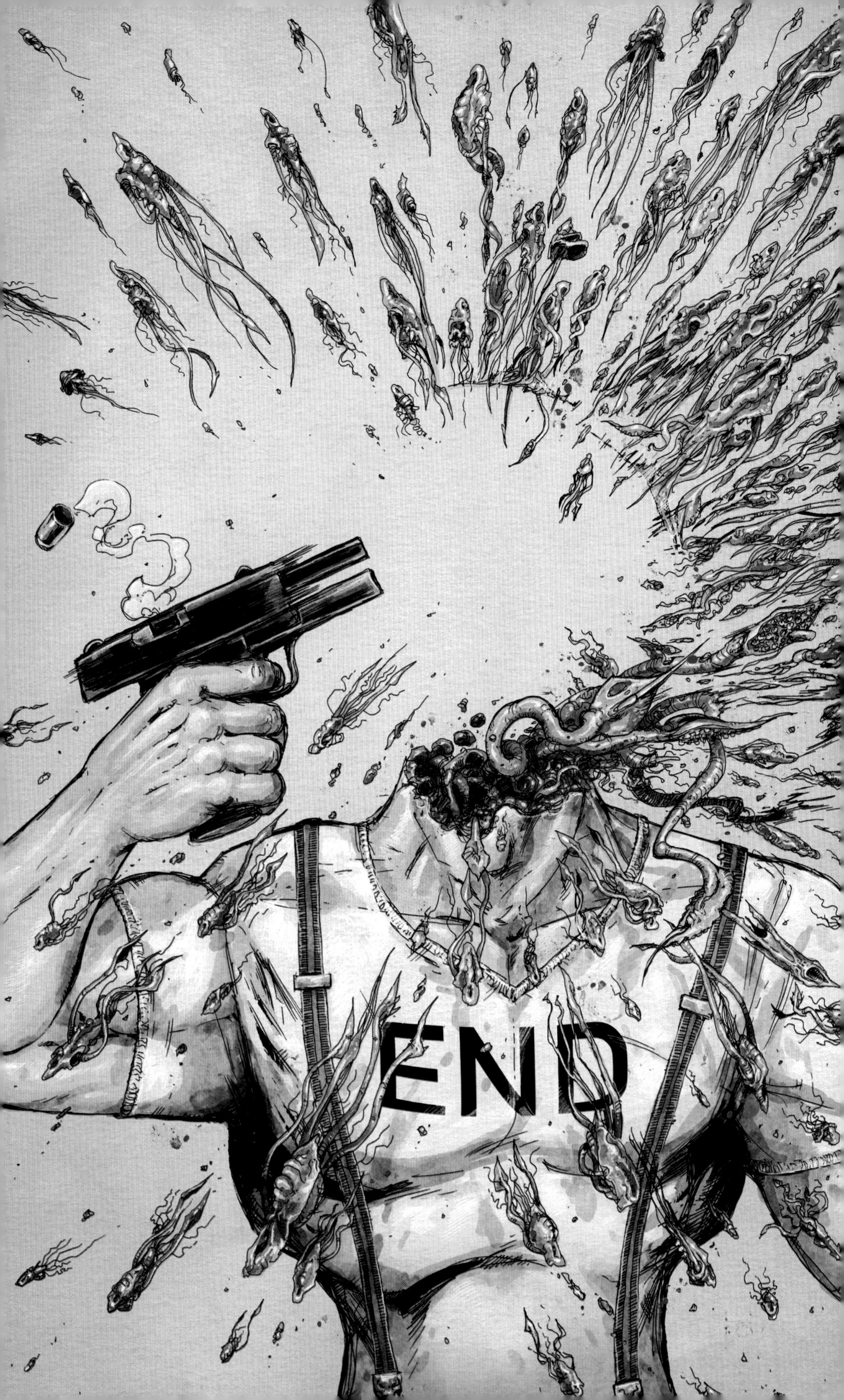
END

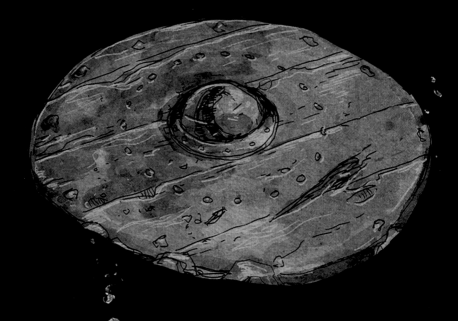

Exhibit 554
Bjarte's Shield

When Egil found Bjarte's shield on the empty battlefield,
he was shaking with giddy joy. But a warrior's shield holds
a warrior's burden and on his way home to show his brother a lone survivor of the battle saw the shield and aimed
for what must be the enemy. Egil's little brother found his
body before sundown and could not think of a way to tell
his mother. He brought her down but the Evorah had already taken everything.

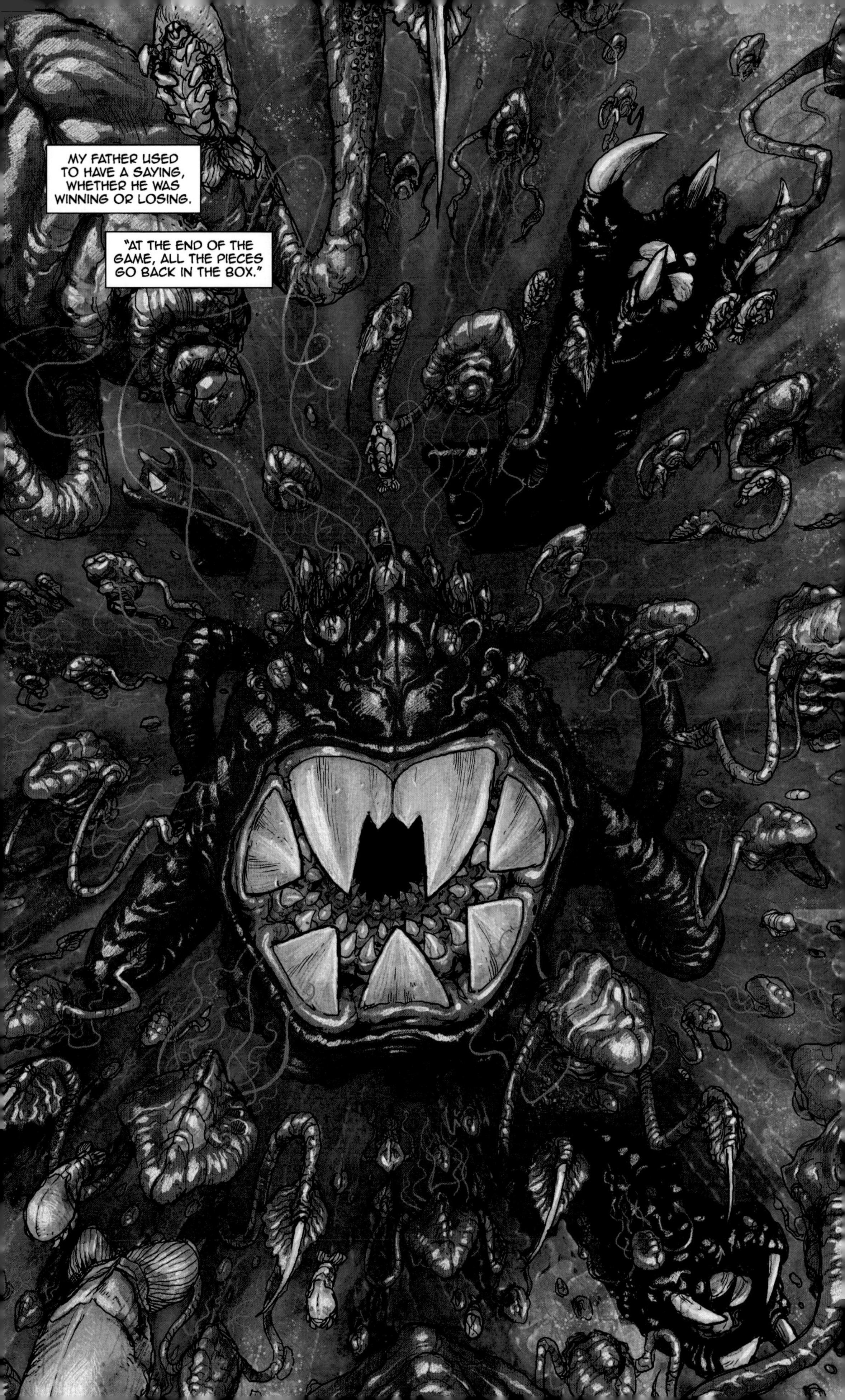
MY FATHER USED TO HAVE A SAYING, WHETHER HE WAS WINNING OR LOSING.
"AT THE END OF THE GAME, ALL THE PIECES GO BACK IN THE BOX."

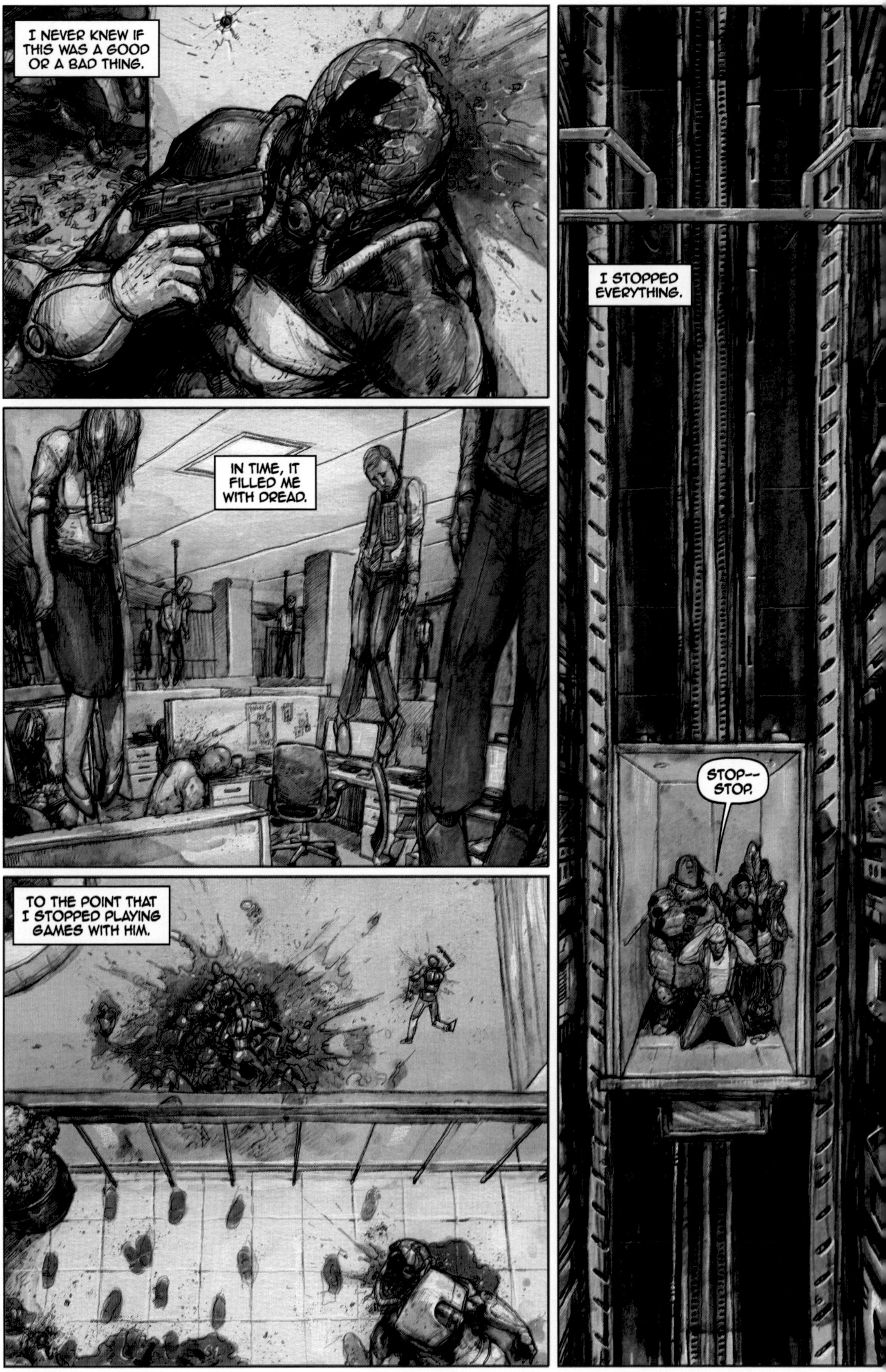
I NEVER KNEW IF THIS WAS A GOOD OR A BAD THING.
IN TIME, IT FILLED ME WITH DREAD.
TO THE POINT THAT I STOPPED PLAYING GAMES WITH HIM.
I STOPPED EVERYTHING.
STOP-- STOP.

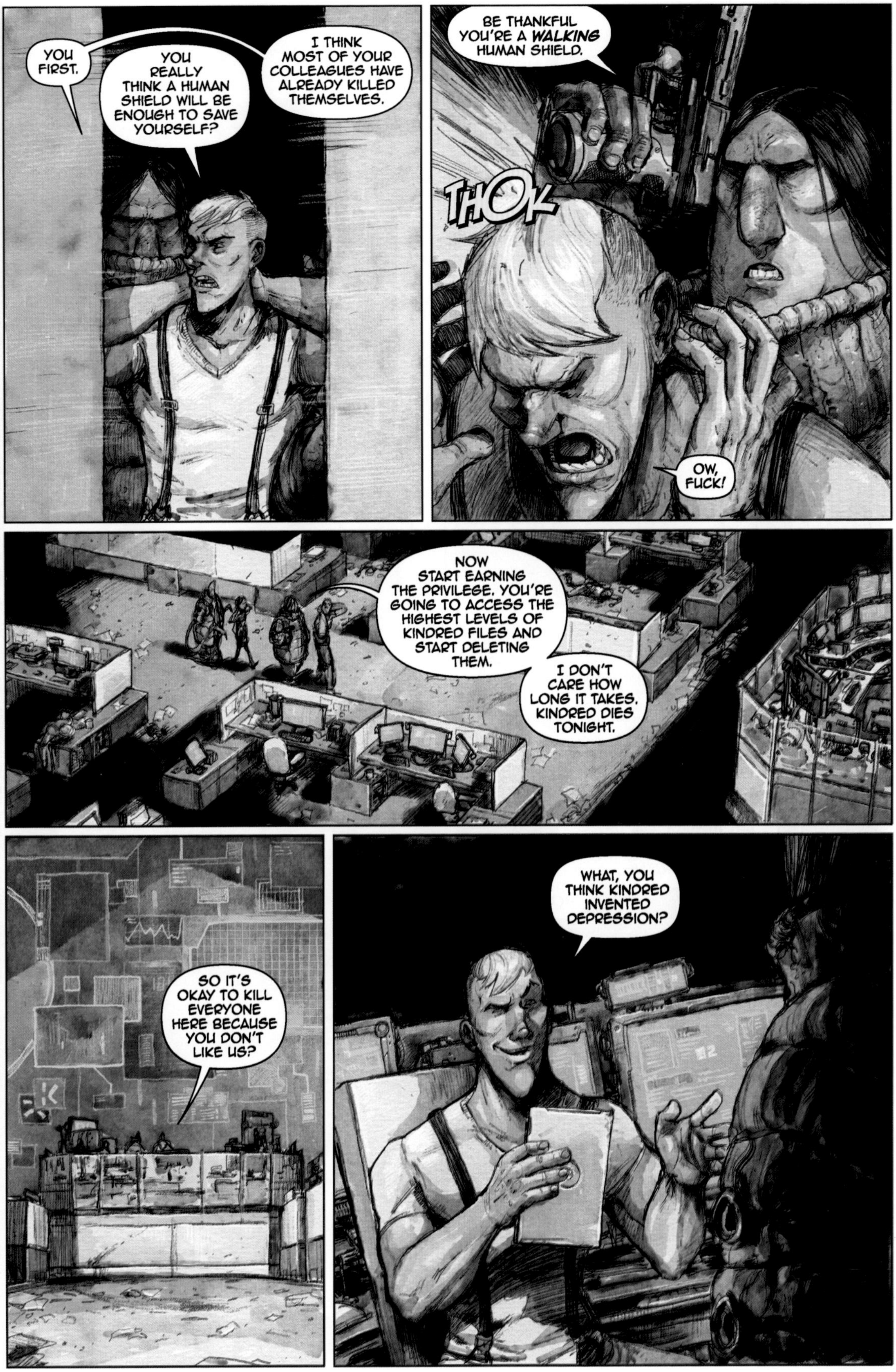
YOU FIRST.
YOU REALLY THINK A HUMAN SHIELD WILL BE ENOUGH TO SAVE YOURSELF?
I THINK MOST OF YOUR COLLEAGUES HAVE ALREADY KILLED THEMSELVES.
BE THANKFUL YOU'RE A *WALKING* HUMAN SHIELD.
THOK
OW, FUCK!
NOW START EARNING THE PRIVILEGE. YOU'RE GOING TO ACCESS THE HIGHEST LEVELS OF KINDRED FILES AND START DELETING THEM.
I DON'T CARE HOW LONG IT TAKES. KINDRED DIES TONIGHT.
SO IT'S OKAY TO KILL EVERYONE HERE BECAUSE YOU DON'T LIKE US?
WHAT, YOU THINK KINDRED INVENTED DEPRESSION?

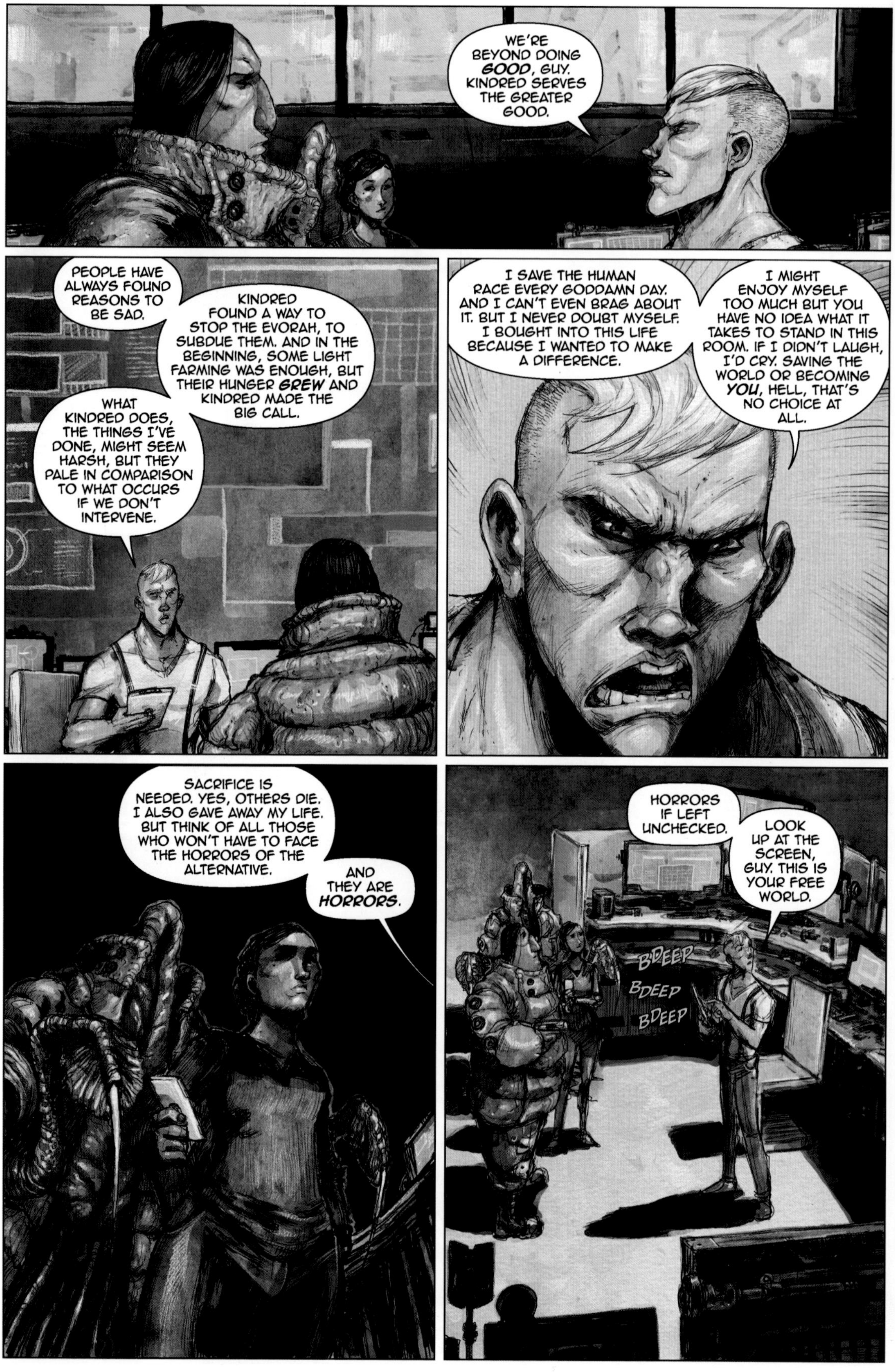
WE'RE BEYOND DOING GOOD, GUY. KINDRED SERVES THE GREATER GOOD.
PEOPLE HAVE ALWAYS FOUND REASONS TO BE SAD.
KINDRED FOUND A WAY TO STOP THE EVORAH, TO SUBDUE THEM. AND IN THE BEGINNING, SOME LIGHT FARMING WAS ENOUGH, BUT THEIR HUNGER GREW AND KINDRED MADE THE BIG CALL.
WHAT KINDRED DOES, THE THINGS I'VE DONE, MIGHT SEEM HARSH, BUT THEY PALE IN COMPARISON TO WHAT OCCURS IF WE DON'T INTERVENE.
I SAVE THE HUMAN RACE EVERY GODDAMN DAY. AND I CAN'T EVEN BRAG ABOUT IT. BUT I NEVER DOUBT MYSELF. I BOUGHT INTO THIS LIFE BECAUSE I WANTED TO MAKE A DIFFERENCE.
I MIGHT ENJOY MYSELF TOO MUCH BUT YOU HAVE NO IDEA WHAT IT TAKES TO STAND IN THIS ROOM. IF I DIDN'T LAUGH, I'D CRY. SAVING THE WORLD OR BECOMING YOU, HELL, THAT'S NO CHOICE AT ALL.
SACRIFICE IS NEEDED. YES, OTHERS DIE. I ALSO GAVE AWAY MY LIFE. BUT THINK OF ALL THOSE WHO WON'T HAVE TO FACE THE HORRORS OF THE ALTERNATIVE.
AND THEY ARE HORRORS.
HORRORS IF LEFT UNCHECKED.
LOOK UP AT THE SCREEN, GUY. THIS IS YOUR FREE WORLD.
BDEEP
BDEEP
BDEEP

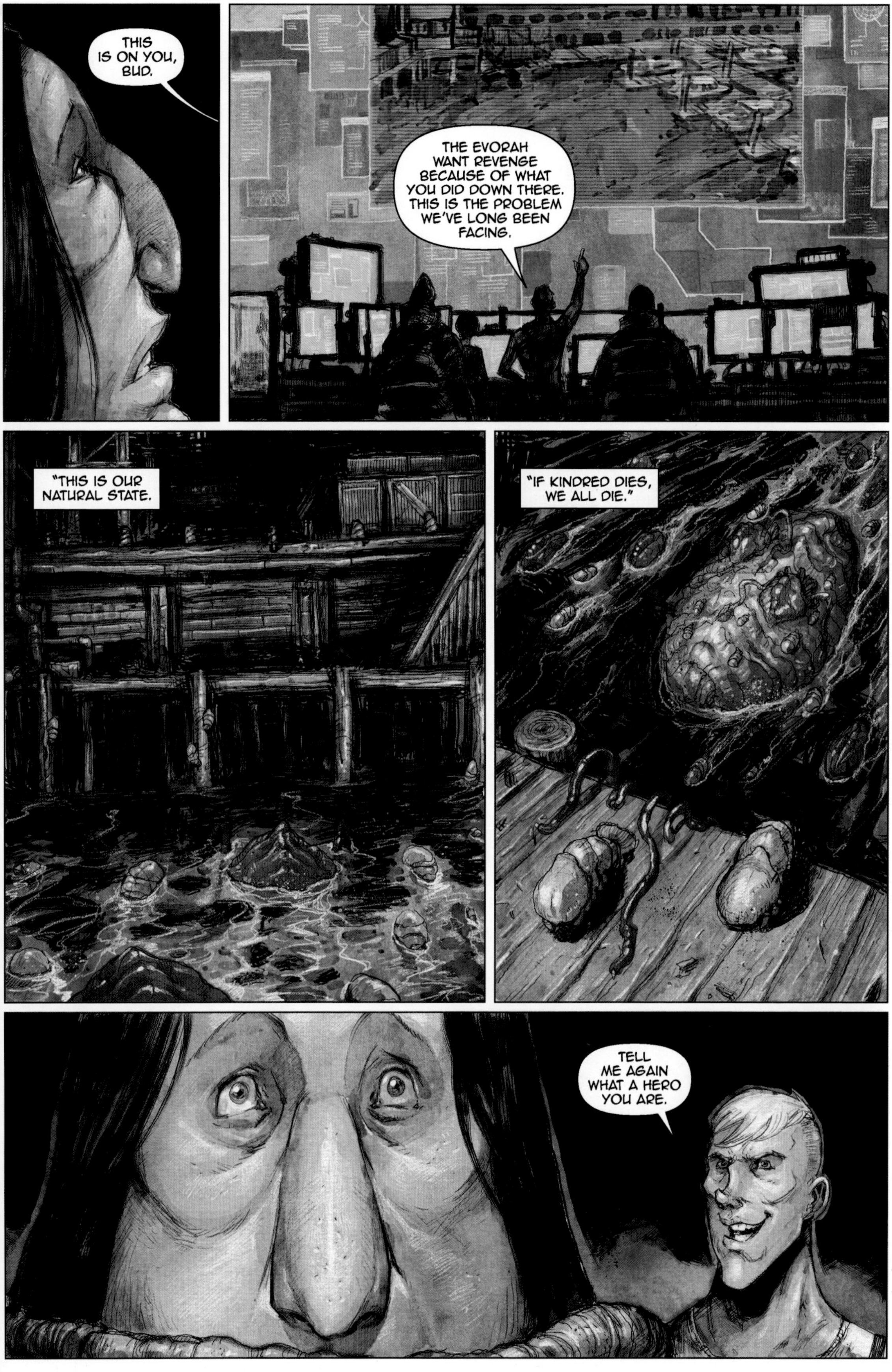
THIS IS ON YOU, BUD.
THE EVORAH WANT REVENGE BECAUSE OF WHAT YOU DID DOWN THERE. THIS IS THE PROBLEM WE'VE LONG BEEN FACING.
"THIS IS OUR NATURAL STATE.
"IF KINDRED DIES, WE ALL DIE."
TELL ME AGAIN WHAT A HERO YOU ARE.

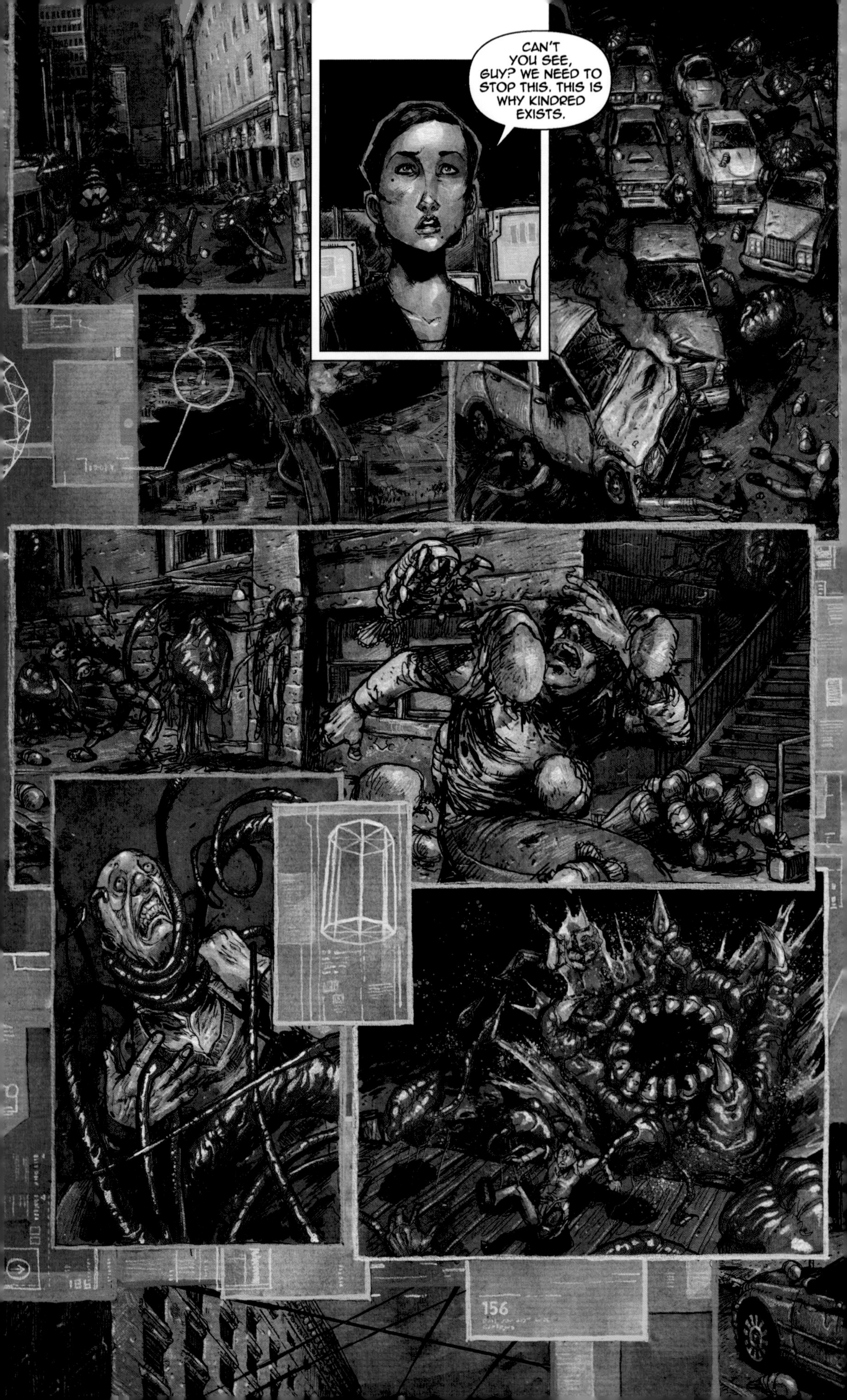
CAN'T YOU SEE, GUY? WE NEED TO STOP THIS. THIS IS WHY KINDRED EXISTS.
156

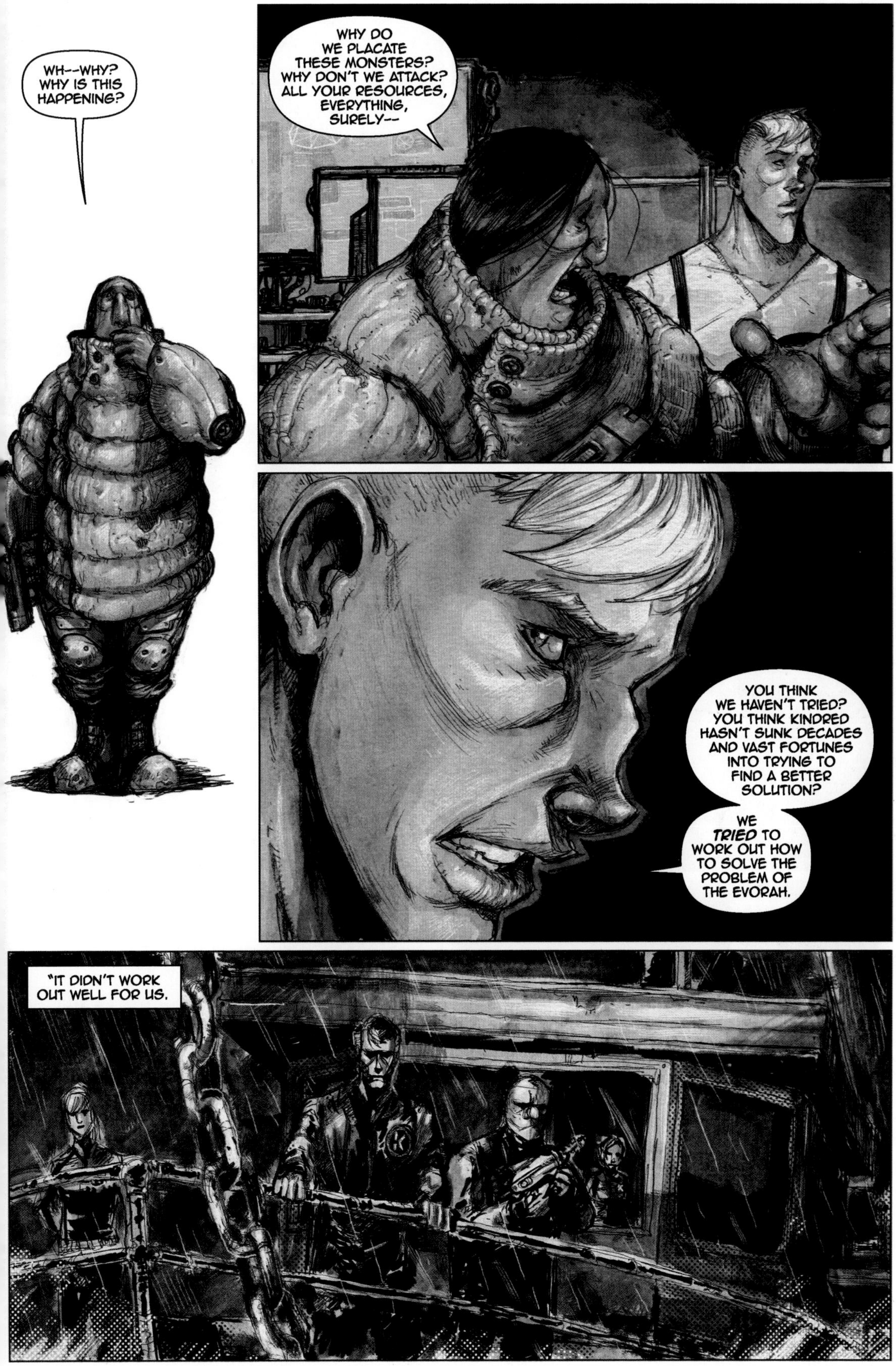
WH--WHY? WHY IS THIS HAPPENING?
WHY DO WE PLACATE THESE MONSTERS? WHY DON'T WE ATTACK? ALL YOUR RESOURCES, EVERYTHING, SURELY--
YOU THINK WE HAVEN'T TRIED? YOU THINK KINDRED HASN'T SUNK DECADES AND VAST FORTUNES INTO TRYING TO FIND A BETTER SOLUTION?
WE *TRIED* TO WORK OUT HOW TO SOLVE THE PROBLEM OF THE EVORAH.
"IT DIDN'T WORK OUT WELL FOR US.

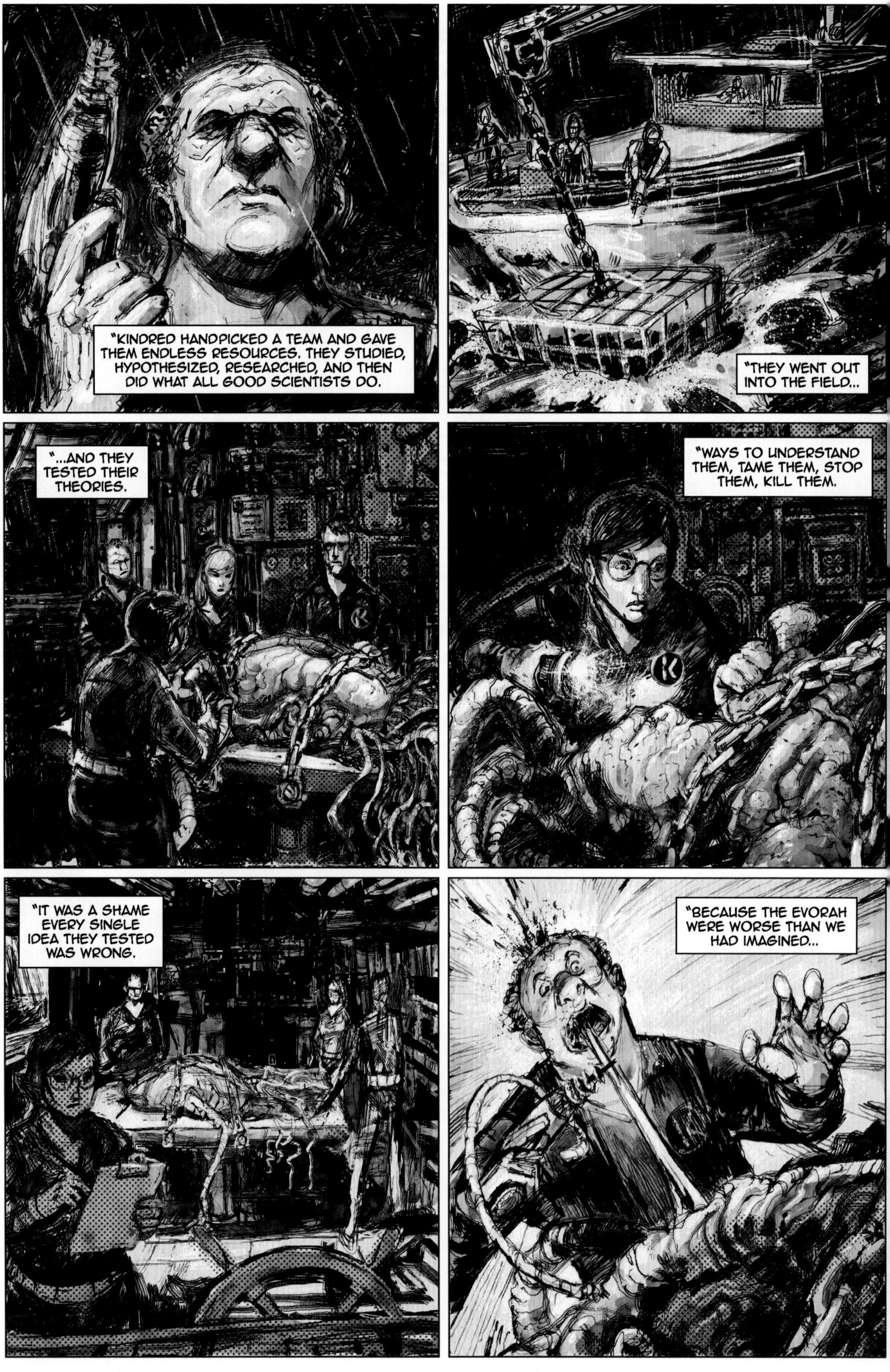
"KINDRED HANDPICKED A TEAM AND GAVE THEM ENDLESS RESOURCES. THEY STUDIED, HYPOTHESIZED, RESEARCHED, AND THEN DID WHAT ALL GOOD SCIENTISTS DO.
"THEY WENT OUT INTO THE FIELD...
"...AND THEY TESTED THEIR THEORIES.
"WAYS TO UNDERSTAND THEM, TAME THEM, STOP THEM, KILL THEM.
"IT WAS A SHAME EVERY SINGLE IDEA THEY TESTED WAS WRONG.
"BECAUSE THE EVORAH WERE WORSE THAN WE HAD IMAGINED...

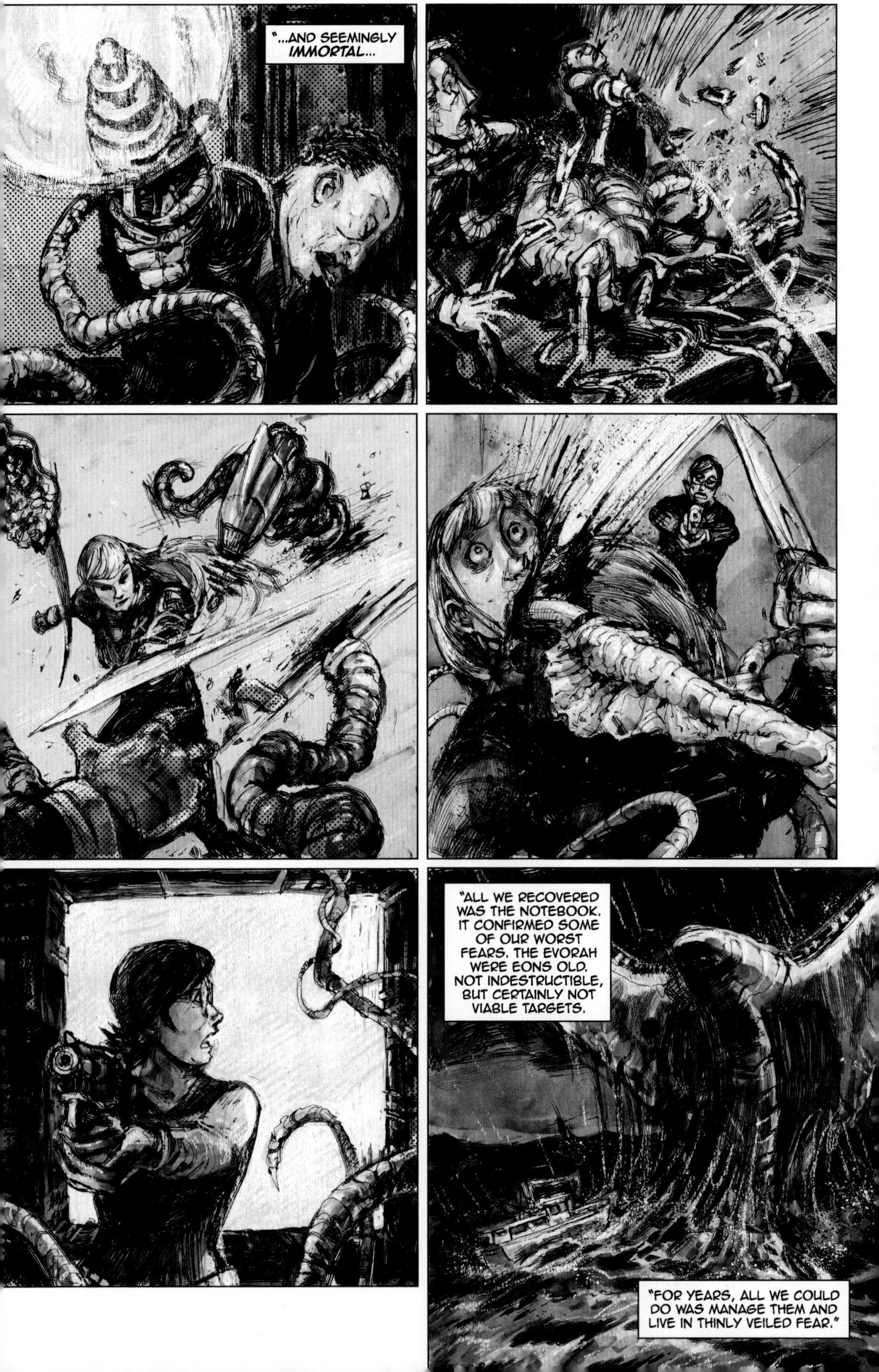
"...AND SEEMINGLY *IMMORTAL*...
"ALL WE RECOVERED WAS THE NOTEBOOK. IT CONFIRMED SOME OF OUR WORST FEARS. THE EVORAH WERE EONS OLD. NOT INDESTRUCTIBLE, BUT CERTAINLY NOT VIABLE TARGETS.
"FOR YEARS, ALL WE COULD DO WAS MANAGE THEM AND LIVE IN THINLY VEILED FEAR."

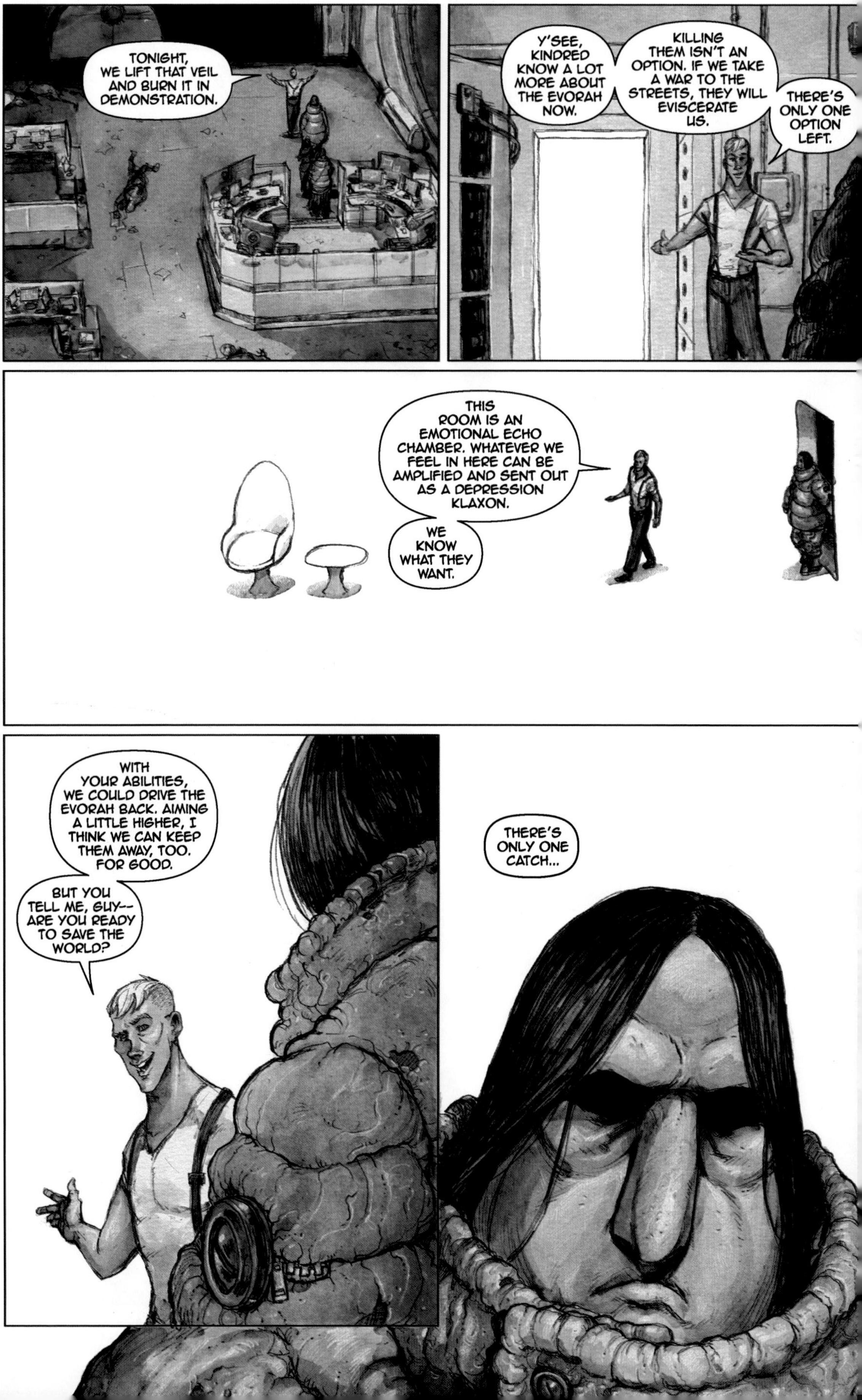
TONIGHT, WE LIFT THAT VEIL AND BURN IT IN DEMONSTRATION.
Y'SEE, KINDRED KNOW A LOT MORE ABOUT THE EVORAH NOW.
KILLING THEM ISN'T AN OPTION. IF WE TAKE A WAR TO THE STREETS, THEY WILL EVISCERATE US.
THERE'S ONLY ONE OPTION LEFT.
THIS ROOM IS AN EMOTIONAL ECHO CHAMBER. WHATEVER WE FEEL IN HERE CAN BE AMPLIFIED AND SENT OUT AS A DEPRESSION KLAXON.
WE KNOW WHAT THEY WANT.
WITH YOUR ABILITIES, WE COULD DRIVE THE EVORAH BACK. AIMING A LITTLE HIGHER, I THINK WE CAN KEEP THEM AWAY, TOO. FOR GOOD.
BUT YOU TELL ME, GUY-- ARE YOU READY TO SAVE THE WORLD?
THERE'S ONLY ONE CATCH...

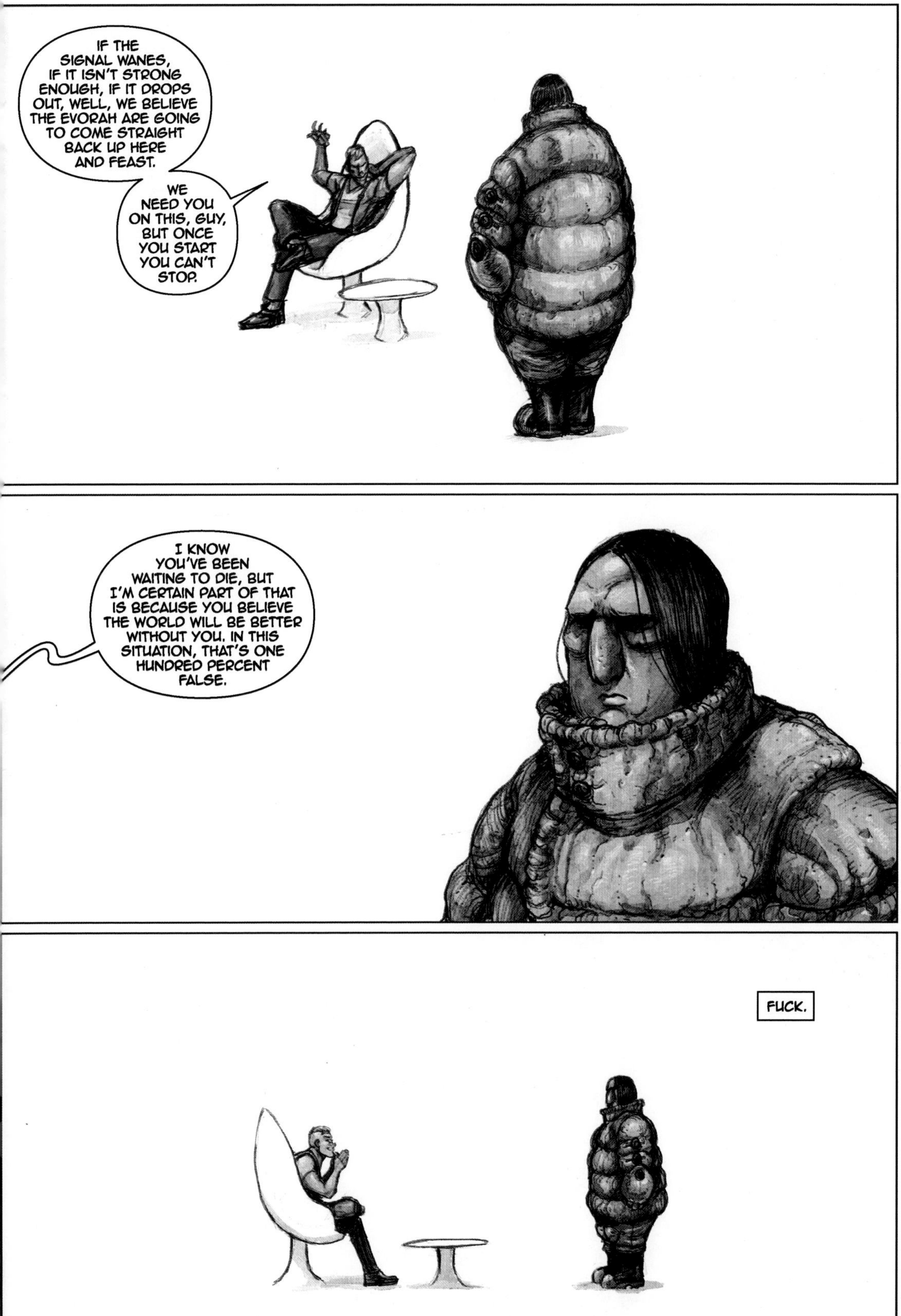
IF THE SIGNAL WANES, IF IT ISN'T STRONG ENOUGH, IF IT DROPS OUT, WELL, WE BELIEVE THE EVORAH ARE GOING TO COME STRAIGHT BACK UP HERE AND FEAST.
WE NEED YOU ON THIS, GUY, BUT ONCE YOU START YOU CAN'T STOP.
I KNOW YOU'VE BEEN WAITING TO DIE, BUT I'M CERTAIN PART OF THAT IS BECAUSE YOU BELIEVE THE WORLD WILL BE BETTER WITHOUT YOU. IN THIS SITUATION, THAT'S ONE HUNDRED PERCENT FALSE.
FUCK.

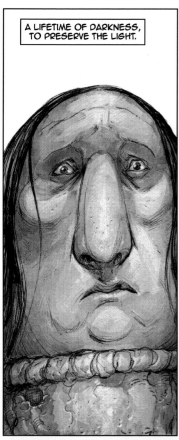

A LIFETIME OF DARKNESS, TO PRESERVE THE LIGHT.

OKAY.

SUPERB!

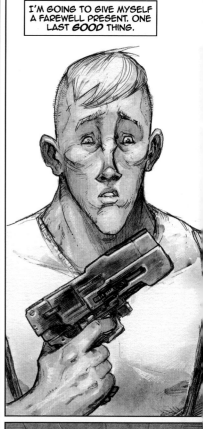

I'M GOING TO GIVE MYSELF A FAREWELL PRESENT. ONE LAST *GOOD* THING.

BLAM

LEAVE HIM IN THERE. ON SOME LEVEL, HE'LL HELP.

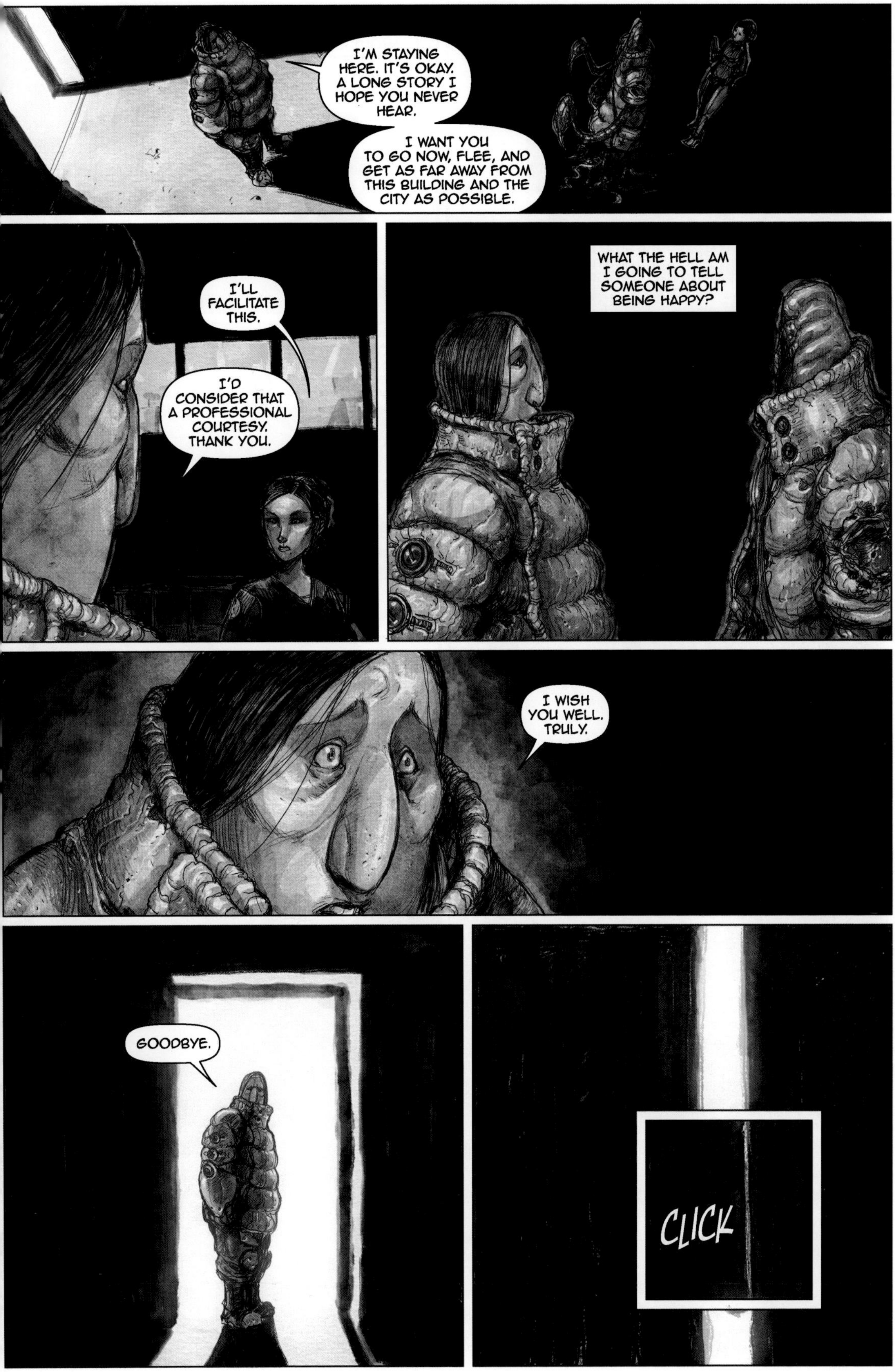

I'M STAYING HERE. IT'S OKAY. A LONG STORY I HOPE YOU NEVER HEAR.
I WANT YOU TO GO NOW, FLEE, AND GET AS FAR AWAY FROM THIS BUILDING AND THE CITY AS POSSIBLE.
I'LL FACILITATE THIS.
I'D CONSIDER THAT A PROFESSIONAL COURTESY. THANK YOU.
WHAT THE HELL AM I GOING TO TELL SOMEONE ABOUT BEING HAPPY?
I WISH YOU WELL. TRULY.
GOODBYE.
CLICK

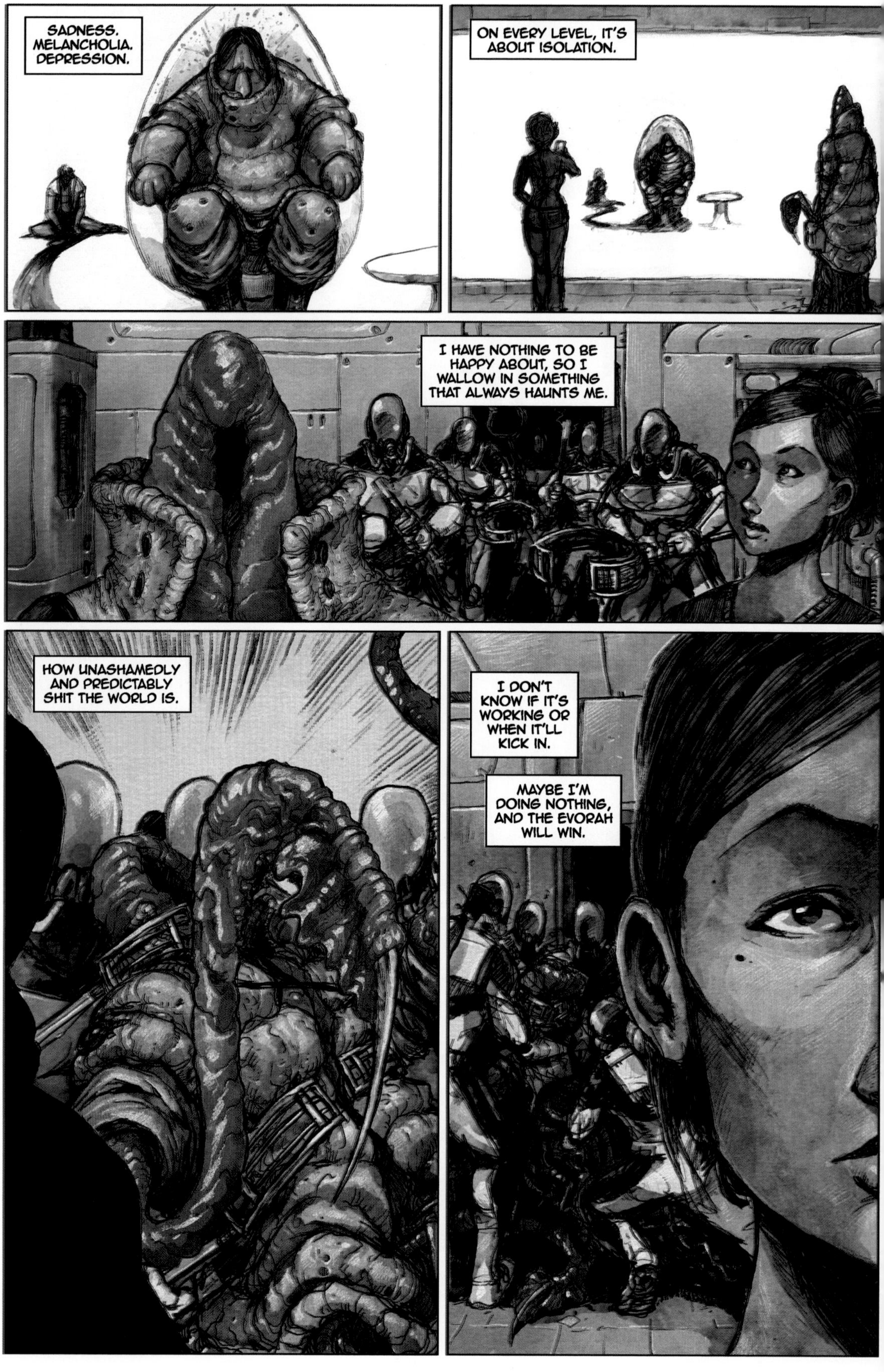
SADNESS. MELANCHOLIA. DEPRESSION.
ON EVERY LEVEL, IT'S ABOUT ISOLATION.
I HAVE NOTHING TO BE HAPPY ABOUT, SO I WALLOW IN SOMETHING THAT ALWAYS HAUNTS ME.
HOW UNASHAMEDLY AND PREDICTABLY SHIT THE WORLD IS.
I DON'T KNOW IF IT'S WORKING OR WHEN IT'LL KICK IN.
MAYBE I'M DOING NOTHING, AND THE EVORAH WILL WIN.

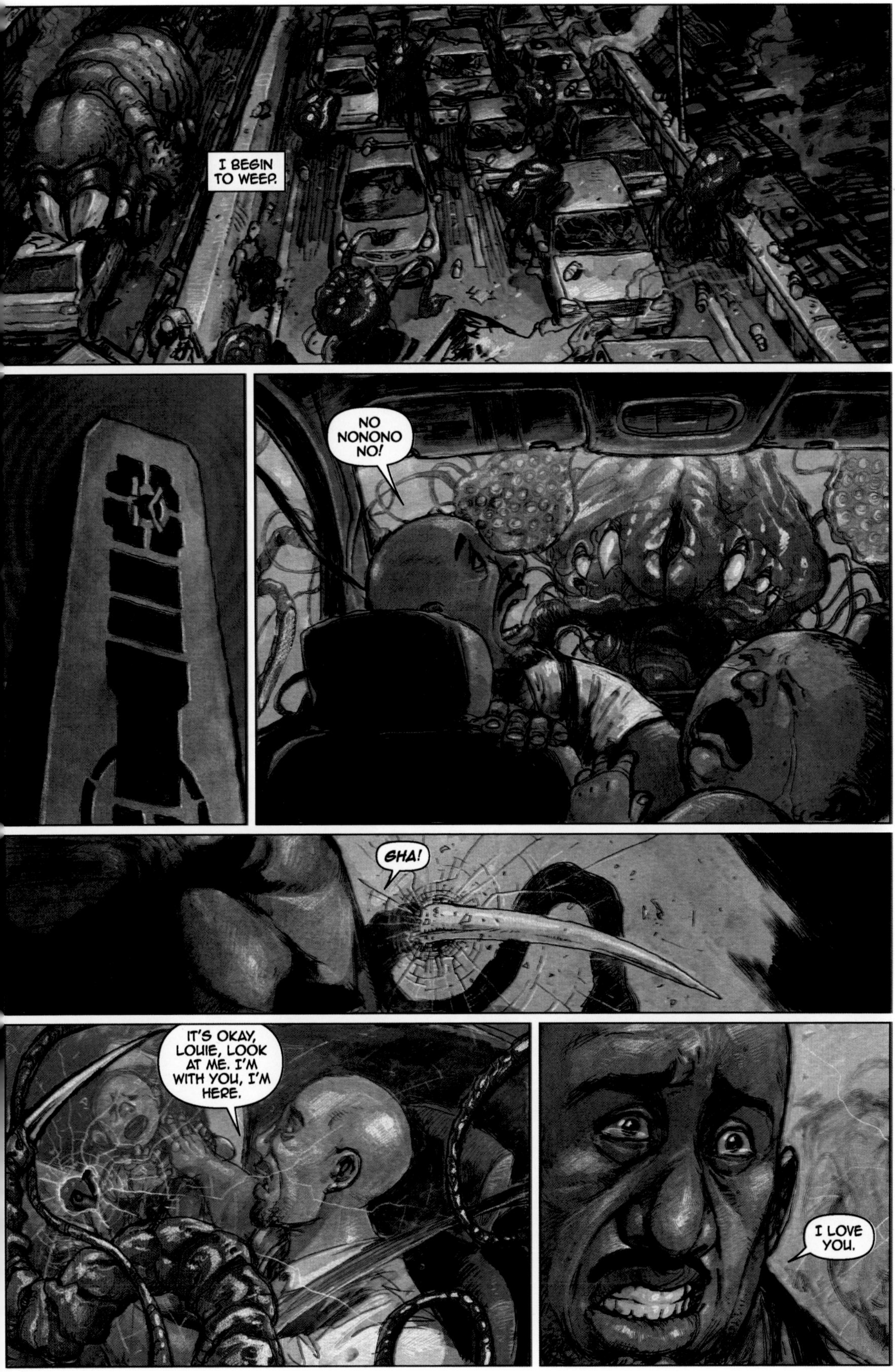
I BEGIN TO WEEP.
NO NONONO NO!
GHA!
IT'S OKAY, LOUIE, LOOK AT ME. I'M WITH YOU, I'M HERE.
I LOVE YOU.

CLOSE YOUR EYES.

THIS'LL ALL BE OVER SOON.

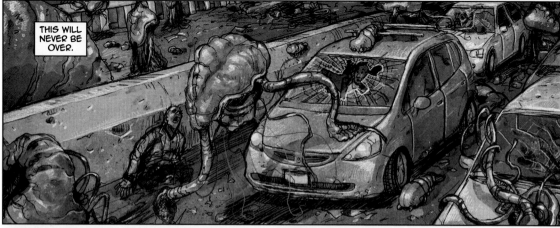

THIS WILL NEVER BE OVER.

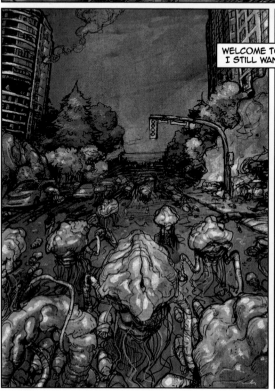

WELCOME TO MY LIFE; I STILL WANT TO DIE.

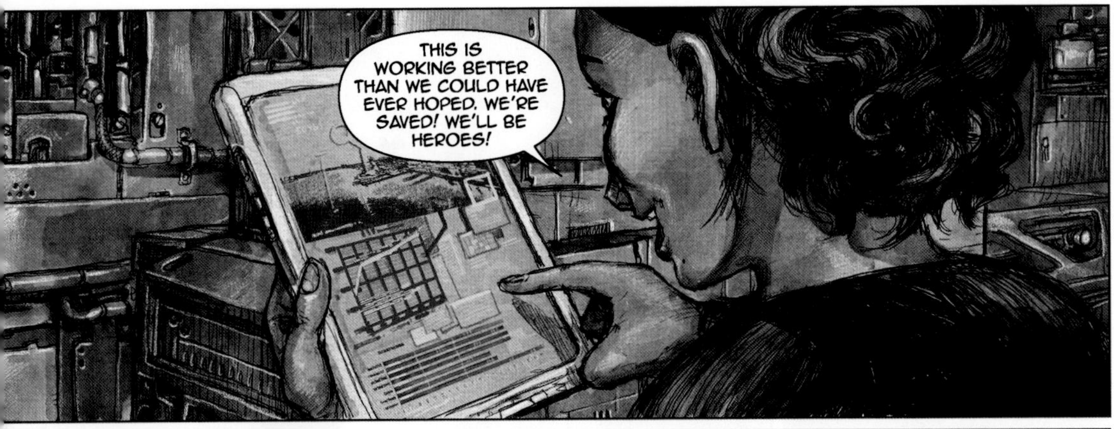
THIS IS WORKING BETTER THAN WE COULD HAVE EVER HOPED. WE'RE SAVED! WE'LL BE HEROES!

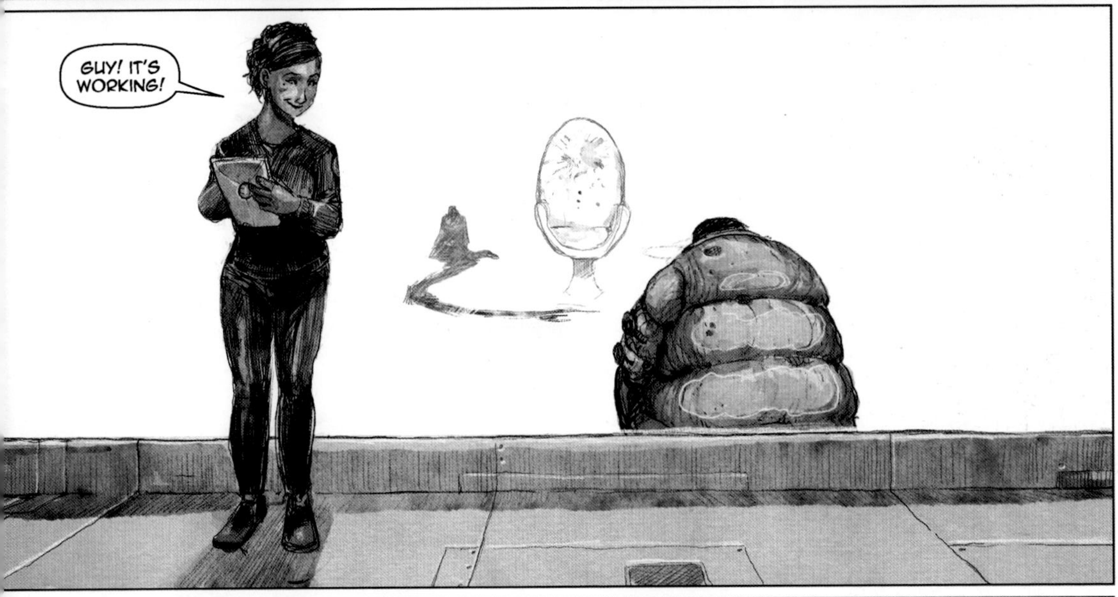
GUY! IT'S WORKING!

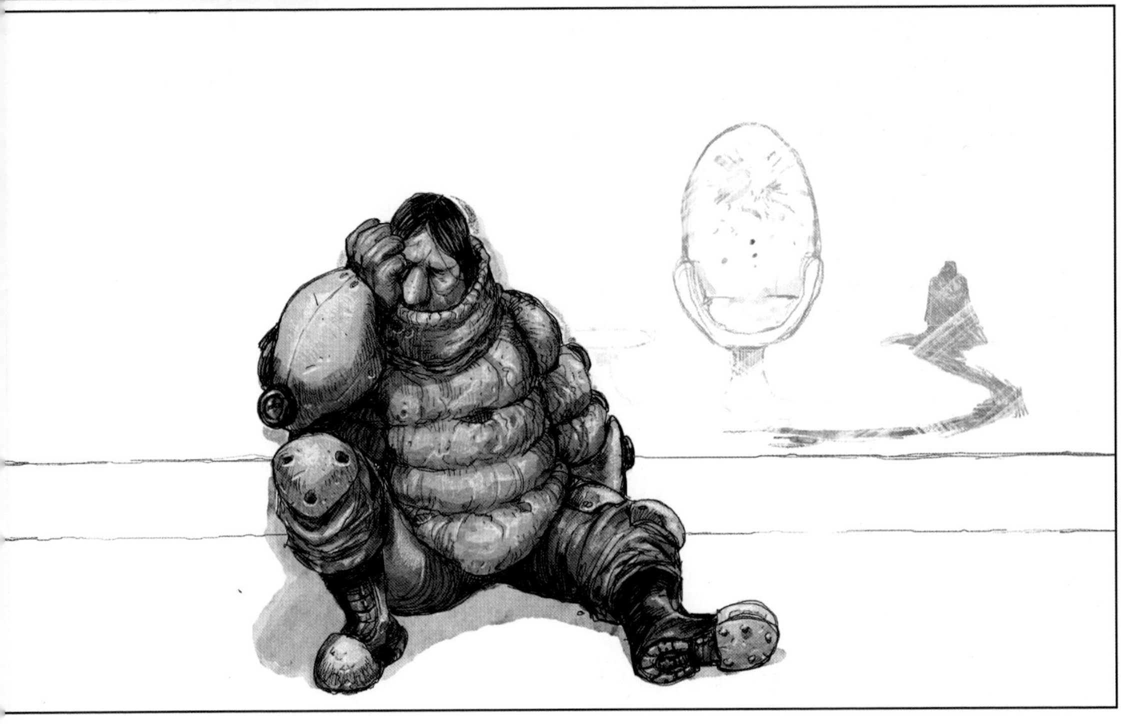

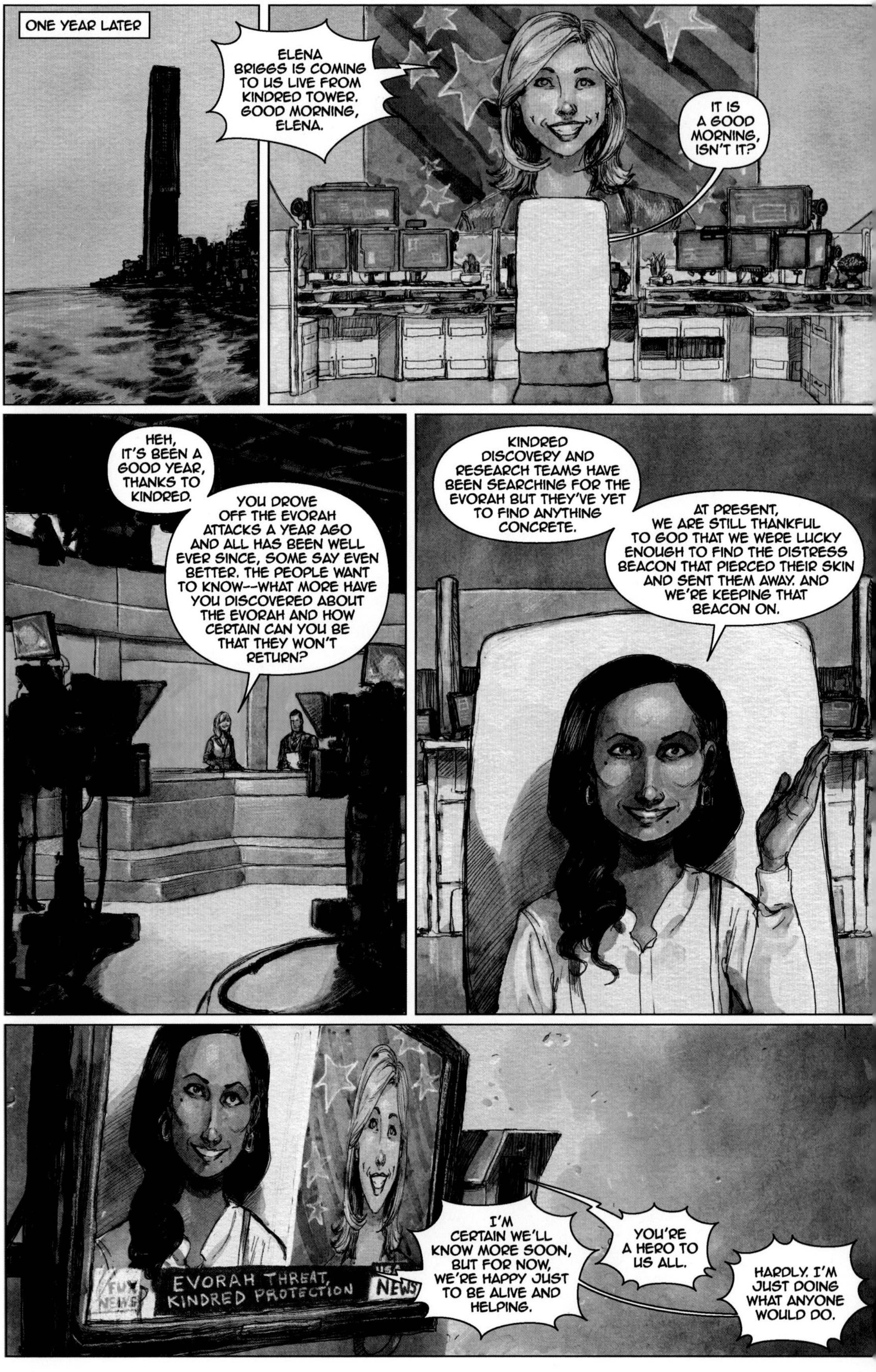

ONE YEAR LATER
ELENA BRIGGS IS COMING TO US LIVE FROM KINDRED TOWER. GOOD MORNING, ELENA.
IT IS A GOOD MORNING, ISN'T IT?
HEH, IT'S BEEN A GOOD YEAR, THANKS TO KINDRED.
YOU DROVE OFF THE EVORAH ATTACKS A YEAR AGO AND ALL HAS BEEN WELL EVER SINCE, SOME SAY EVEN BETTER. THE PEOPLE WANT TO KNOW--WHAT MORE HAVE YOU DISCOVERED ABOUT THE EVORAH AND HOW CERTAIN CAN YOU BE THAT THEY WON'T RETURN?
KINDRED DISCOVERY AND RESEARCH TEAMS HAVE BEEN SEARCHING FOR THE EVORAH BUT THEY'VE YET TO FIND ANYTHING CONCRETE.
AT PRESENT, WE ARE STILL THANKFUL TO GOD THAT WE WERE LUCKY ENOUGH TO FIND THE DISTRESS BEACON THAT PIERCED THEIR SKIN AND SENT THEM AWAY. AND WE'RE KEEPING THAT BEACON ON.
EVORAH THREAT, KINDRED PROTECTION
NEWS
I'M CERTAIN WE'LL KNOW MORE SOON, BUT FOR NOW, WE'RE HAPPY JUST TO BE ALIVE AND HELPING.
YOU'RE A HERO TO US ALL.
HARDLY. I'M JUST DOING WHAT ANYONE WOULD DO.

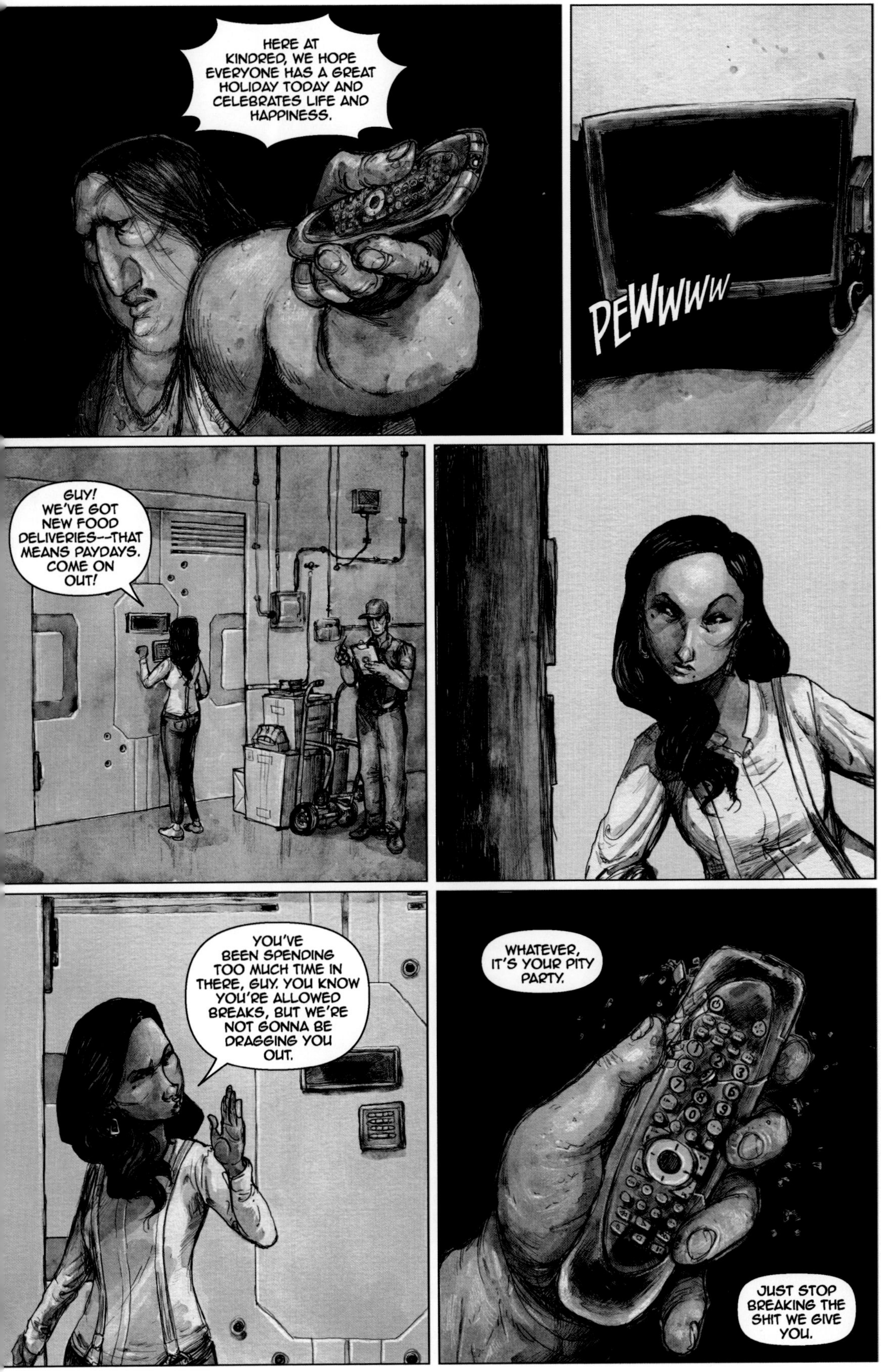
HERE AT KINDRED, WE HOPE EVERYONE HAS A GREAT HOLIDAY TODAY AND CELEBRATES LIFE AND HAPPINESS.
PEWWWW
GUY! WE'VE GOT NEW FOOD DELIVERIES--THAT MEANS PAYDAYS. COME ON OUT!
YOU'VE BEEN SPENDING TOO MUCH TIME IN THERE, GUY. YOU KNOW YOU'RE ALLOWED BREAKS, BUT WE'RE NOT GONNA BE DRAGGING YOU OUT.
WHATEVER, IT'S YOUR PITY PARTY.
JUST STOP BREAKING THE SHIT WE GIVE YOU.

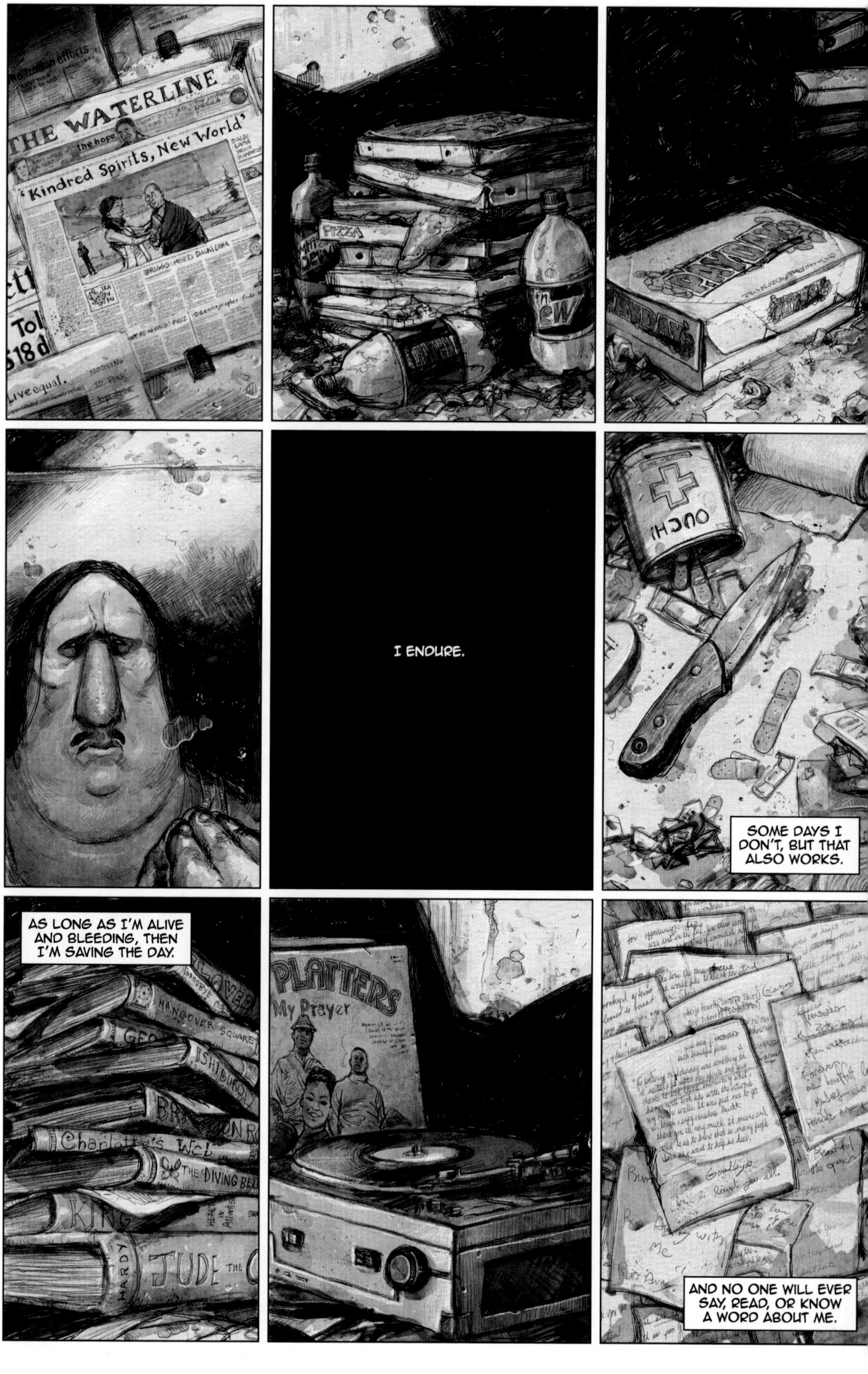
THE WATERLINE
'Kindred Spirits, New World'
PIZZA
I ENDURE.
OUCH
SOME DAYS I DON'T, BUT THAT ALSO WORKS.
AS LONG AS I'M ALIVE AND BLEEDING, THEN I'M SAVING THE DAY.
HANGOVER SQUARE
Charlotte's Web
THE DIVING BELL
HARDY
JUDE THE
PLATTERS
My Prayer
AND NO ONE WILL EVER SAY, READ, OR KNOW A WORD ABOUT ME.

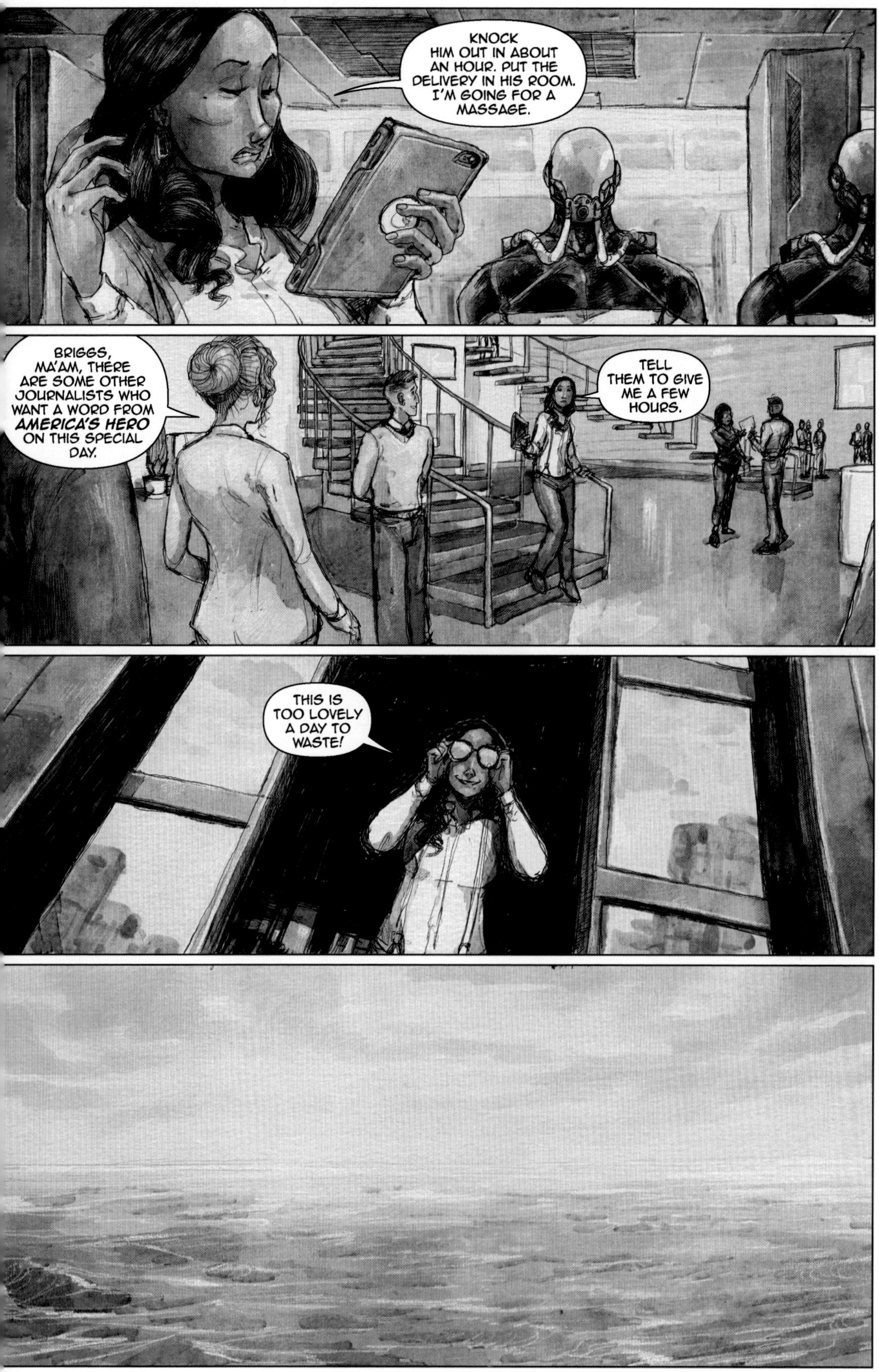
KNOCK HIM OUT IN ABOUT AN HOUR. PUT THE DELIVERY IN HIS ROOM. I'M GOING FOR A MASSAGE.
BRIGGS, MA'AM, THERE ARE SOME OTHER JOURNALISTS WHO WANT A WORD FROM *AMERICA'S HERO* ON THIS SPECIAL DAY.
TELL THEM TO GIVE ME A FEW HOURS.
THIS IS TOO LOVELY A DAY TO WASTE!

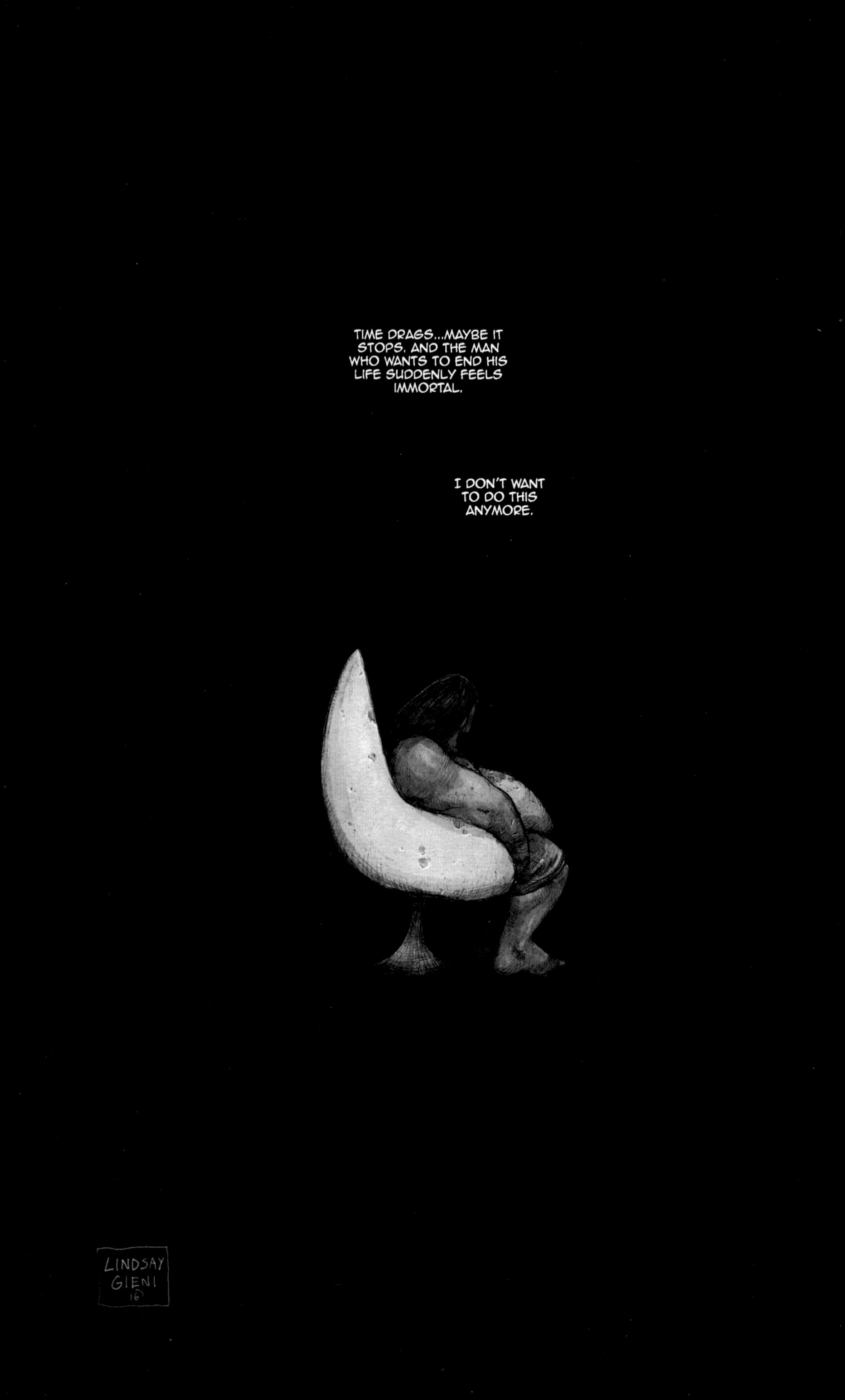
TIME DRAGS...MAYBE IT STOPS. AND THE MAN WHO WANTS TO END HIS LIFE SUDDENLY FEELS IMMORTAL.
I DON'T WANT TO DO THIS ANYMORE.
LINDSAY GIENI 16

GOODBYE...

...NO.

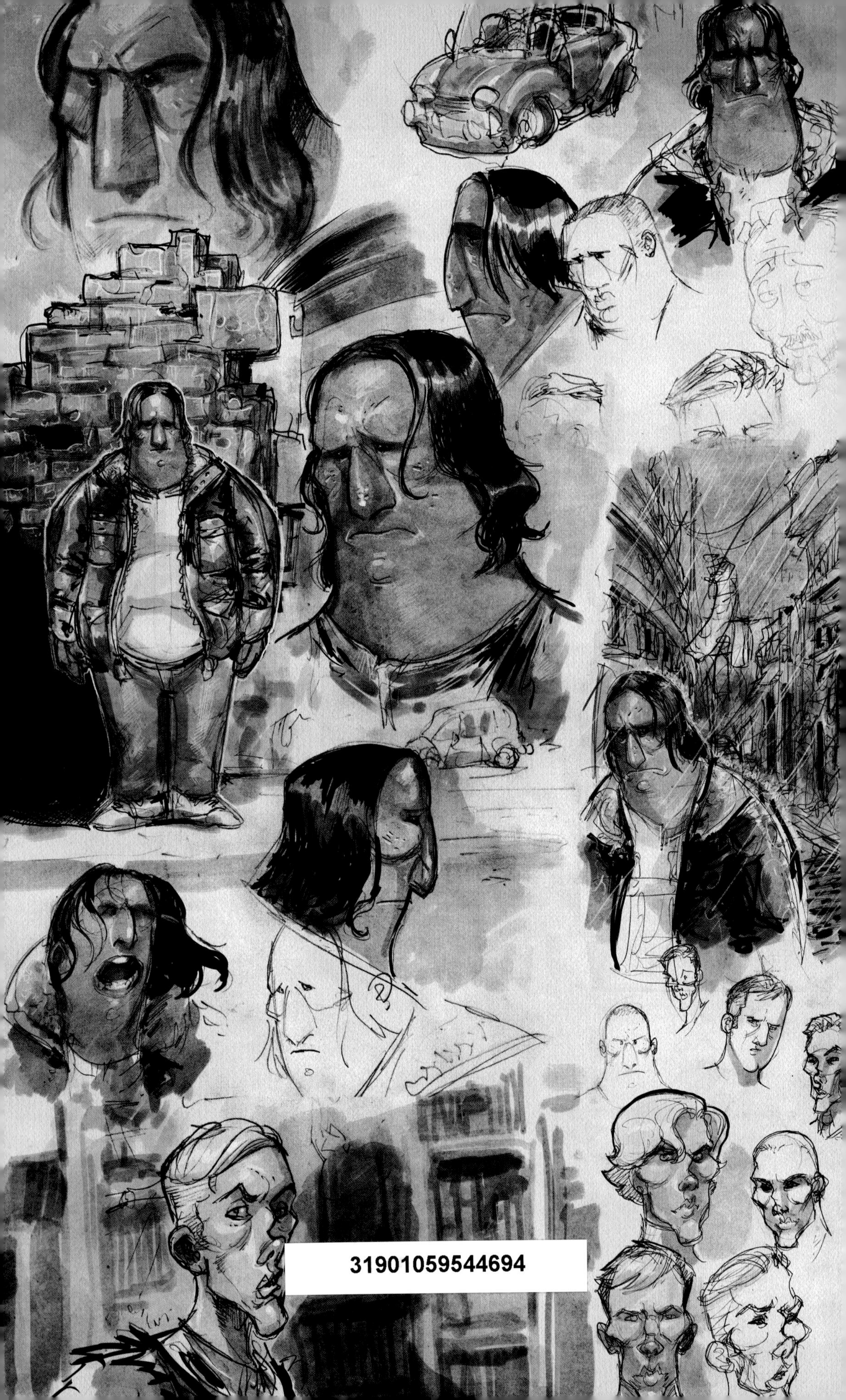